D0864950

Journalism
A Career Handbook

Anna McKane

London: A & C Black,
2004

0713667966

A & C Black · London

Published 2004
A & C Black Publishers Ltd
37 Soho Square
London W1D 3QZ
www.acblack.com

© Anna McKane 2004

ISBN 0-7136-6796-6

A CIP catalogue record for this book is available from the British Library

A & C Black uses paper produced with elemental chlorine-free pulp, harvested
from managed sustainable forests.

Printed and bound in Great Britain
by Creative Print and Design (Wales), Ebbw Vale

Contents

Foreword

The transformation of journalism from a rather rough-and-ready trade into something like a profession has been a slow process, not least in terms of educational standards. When I left school in 1962 to take up a job as a cub reporter on a local weekly newspaper, I was obliged to work a six-month probationary period to ascertain whether I was suitable to be an indentured apprentice journalist. Once I signed up for my three-year apprenticeship, the major educational requirement was attendance at a college once a week to learn shorthand, law, the British constitution, advanced English and, supposedly, 'practical journalism'. On-the-job training tended to be of the sink-or-swim variety but the editor was free with advice – even if I foolishly ignored most of it – and my two reporting colleagues, who were just a little older than me and only slightly more experienced, were also liberal with it.

At the time, all three of us young wannabes from the *Barking Advertiser* were less than enamoured of the day-release training at West Ham College of Further Education. Hindsight suggests that we were wrong because the course, overseen by the National Council for the Training of Journalists (NCTJ), was sensible. The teachers, whom I remember affectionately, were knowledgeable and conscientious. The central problem was a lack of enthusiasm among us students and there was a good reason for our apathy. We understood that the course culminated in a set of final exams which, if we passed, would gain us the NCTJ proficiency certificate, the industry's standard qualification and supposedly necessary for us to advance further in our careers. But within months of becoming journalists, we learned that national newspaper owners and editors couldn't give a fig for qualifications. Since Fleet Street was our goal it seemed pointless to work for a certificate. Indeed, many regional groups also ignored the NCTJ's certificate: at the end of my indentures, despite having failed one part of the exam, I was taken on by the editor of an evening paper owned by one of Britain's largest chains.

Therefore it was the industry's leading newspaper owners who undermined both the theory and practice of a journalistic education they affected to support. Some forty years on I would like to report that the situation has changed. I'm sorry to say that it hasn't because there is still no formal recognition by owners and editors. The current picture is not nearly as bleak as it would seem, however, because there is no doubt that there is an informal acceptance of educational qualifications of a far higher standard than previously. Editors now expect that almost all the people who apply to them for jobs will have a university degree. Some, though not enough, also demand a level of journalistic training too.

In fairness, there have also been weaknesses in the NCTJ system. But, as this book points out, the NCTJ may be on the verge of sorting itself out: it's in a period of transition under a thoughtful and energetic new chief executive. So there is a glimmer of hope that we are on the final road towards the establishment of a set of educational and professional standards for what is now rightly regarded as a profession. This understanding of journalism's improved status is one of this book's underlying themes and strengths. It also recognises that journalism of all kinds – newspaper, magazine, on-line, whether as reporter, sub-editor, photographer or designer – stems from the same essential requirement: to tell the world as honestly as possible about as many subjects as possible.

Hopeful print journalists will find this an eminently sensible and comprehensive guide, providing the kind of valuable 'insider' information which will enable them to take rational decisions about their futures. It is also enlivened by the experiences of journalism students who have taken that all-important first step on the career ladder. I cannot recommend it too highly.

Roy Greenslade
Professor of Journalism, City University

Acknowledgements

Thanks to all those, too many to list, who gave me all sorts of information and background, but special thanks to the following friends and colleagues for help with facts, impressions, advice and ideas: Melanie McFadyean, Harriett Gilbert, James Anslow, Barbara Rowlands, Barbara Norden (especially for her original list of books by journalists), Andrew Grant Adamson, Barbara Schofield, Neil Thurman, Ivan Barnes, Jonathan Pugh, David Driver and Andy Moger; to Jessica Hodge for help with the original idea and plan, and to Judith Millidge for editing the manuscript; to Christopher McKane, for facts and ideas, and for regularly cooking dinner.

Thanks to past and present students, in company with whom I discovered much of what I know about careers in journalism, and everything I know about football.

Note on gender
To avoid repetitions of the clumsy phrase 'he or she', I have so far as possible alternated 'he' and 'she' throughout the book. There are some areas of journalism where there are more women, particularly consumer magazines and features desks, but men are breaking in there, just as women are breaking into the final male bastion, the sports departments.

Working in Print Journalism

- *What do journalists do?*
- *What are journalists like?*
- *What qualities do you need to be a journalist?*
- *How does the job operate?*
- *Salaries*

'The only qualities essential for real success in journalism are a rat-like cunning, a plausible manner, and a little literary ability.'

Nicholas Tomalin, *Stop the Press,
I Want to Get On*, in *The Sunday Times*, 1969

Estimates for the number of people working as print journalists in Britain today vary wildly. It seems likely that there are about 60,000 to 70,000 people involved more or less full time in print journalism, but there must be several thousand more who are slightly on the fringes, producing material for websites, travel brochures and the like. There are many graphic designers working for pressure groups, charities and firms, who would not regard themselves exactly as journalists but are doing a journalistic-type job. There are many more who do bits of journalism alongside their main job, because they have some expertise in an area, or because they know an editor. The field is expanding at present and there are expected to be several thousand more jobs in print and broadcast journalism in the next decade or so.

What do journalists do?

Journalism is about finding things out: the facts of a plane crash, the outcome of a court case, the latest attempts at spin-doctoring, David Beckham's new hairstyle. Then the idea is to tell as many other people as possible. Generally, this process will be a joint effort, with reporters doing the finding out, photographers taking a picture which makes a point, and the production team getting the material from them to the reader.

One misapprehension about journalists among the general public is that they all write articles. This is a word, incidentally, that few journalists ever use. They either talk about a story, a feature, or simply a 'piece'. All this is known collectively as **copy**. But there are thousands of successful journalists around who have never written a story. For every single reporter whose name appears at the top of a story in a local or national paper, there is another journalist working behind the scenes, having ideas for articles, commissioning them, editing them, designing pages, finding or commissioning the right pictures, and organising production schedules. Those who have not seen it done often cannot understand the amount of work involved in actually converting a list of news stories and features into the newspaper or magazine itself.

Often someone will say, 'I think I would make a good journalist because everyone tells me my writing is good.' It is sad, but true, that in the lower echelons of newspapers and magazines, an interest in 'literary writing' may be a hindrance. There is a story about the playwright Tom Stoppard who was sent to cover an accident when he was a young reporter in Bristol. He wrote a beautiful piece about the atmosphere, the lowering sky, etc, but didn't secure the exact facts of how the crash happened, how many people were injured, and so on. No surprise, then, that he didn't make it as a news reporter, but there is no question about his ability to write.

It is far more important, in the early stages at least, simply to be efficient. A junior reporter needs a clear idea of the facts needed for a news report, a methodical mind to record them accurately, the organisational ability to get back to the office in time and type something into the computer, and the common sense to acquire the phone number of someone who knows what happened. Then the reporter needs charm, so that when she is writing up the story and finds some vital point has been forgotten, she can ring that person up to check it.

Journalists are happiest when they are the first to find something out, and the first to tell everyone else about it. So another quality they either have when they start, or they develop if they do the job well, is a competitive streak. But again this applies to most careers, from medical researchers to teachers. It is probably just a bit more obvious with journalists.

Journalists like to 'Be There'. Some years ago the entire picture team of *The Independent* – picture editors, researchers, staff photographers and freelances – were at a party in Islington. A terrorist bomb went off at the Honourable Artillery Company building in City Road, just near the paper's offices. A duty officer rang the picture editor, and the partygoers heard of the explosion within seconds. The freelance photographers left *en masse*, abandoning half-eaten barbecue, half-drunk glasses and half-drunk and slightly irritated girlfriends.

Some of the photographers were inside the damaged building before the police. One of them, Jon Jones, now a highly successful international photographer, got the picture that was used in the next edition of the paper. Within an hour all the photographers had returned to carry on partying, but one probably echoed all their feelings. He knew he hadn't got the best photo, because Jon Jones got into the building first. 'But,' he grinned happily, '*I was there.*'

The staff photographers didn't dash off to City Road. More secure in their jobs, most had not taken their cameras to a Saturday night party. But the freelances, who cannot afford to miss a chance, had theirs.

Most journalists agree that the job can often be great fun. Meeting people, digging up information, taking a photograph which encapsulates an important story, producing a good-looking paper, magazine or website – all these are creative activities, and from the *Blue Peter* of childhood onwards, most people like creating things. Journalists might moan a lot, but that may be because many of them talk a lot. The other day I was chatting to an older hack whose career has included work on nearly half Britain's national newspapers. It was all fun, he said, but the best fun was being there at the launch of *The Independent*. The arrival of new technology which made the project feasible, the rise of anti-

Murdoch feeling in Britain following his move to Wapping which meant that a good percentage of *Times* readers were looking for a change, and a genuine belief in the paper meant that the first couple of years of its life are regarded by those who were there as having been a golden springtime.

What are journalists like?

'Quoyle, you got some kind of a wreck to brighten the front page?'

E. Annie Proulx, *The Shipping News*

There are a number of misconceptions about what it takes to be a successful journalist, and what it is like being one. Journalists have traditionally been regarded as slightly raffish, maybe a bit loud, perhaps a little untrustworthy. This is not entirely justified. Journalists who break genuine confidences, name a source when they had promised not to do so, or who pretend to be a sheikh when they really work for a Sunday tabloid, are a very small minority, though they are the ones people hear about. As other groups, including politicians, lawyers, even the police, are falling slightly in the public's estimation of their trustworthiness, journalists are being seen as perhaps no worse than anyone else.

Journalists are regarded as glamorous. This image is fuelled by novels, plays and films, and by the elevation of some of them, TV journalists in particular, into media stars. It is an image encouraged by some journalists themselves, who as a group possibly tend to sound off more in the pub about the exciting moments in their work.

Plenty of it is exciting too, but not necessarily in the way non-journalists would expect. It is not all about exposing a crooked tycoon or a bent politician, or uncovering a terrible injustice. Production journalists, for instance, get a kick out of getting a massive national paper, with its endless sections of news and features, to print on time. Gossip columnists would be equally excited about being the first to report on a new romance between two soap stars.

The desire to tell other people things certainly does seem to extend to their workplaces more than with some other walks of life. The image of colleagues and rivals gathering in the pub after work, going over the day and generally gossiping about what has gone on, who is about to be hired or fired, is probably more true of journalists than other professional groups.

Another impression, again gleaned from films and novels, is that journalists are hard-bitten, slightly callous and uncaring. And there is no doubt that some journalists have made their friends wince with their open cynicism. Edward Behr, in his autobiography about his life as a foreign correspondent covering wars and uprisings all over the world, describes a scene in Africa. Belgian refugees were huddled in aircraft hangars waiting to be flown out of the newly-independent Belgian Congo: 'Into the middle of the crowd strode an unmistakeably British TV reporter, leading his cameraman and sundry technicians like a platoon commander through hostile territory. At intervals he paused and shouted, in a stentorian but genteel BBC voice, "Anyone here been raped and speaks English?"' Behr used that cringe-making quote for the title of his book.

Such anecdotes are not likely to improve the standing of journalists, but it may be that journalists are no more cynical than other groups. A vicar I overheard at a dinner party was clearly scandalised to hear a night editor say, with mild satisfaction, that 'Rudolph Nureyev died in time for the edition'. Maybe it was a bit naïve to imagine that a non-journalist would understand the kick the night editor got of getting the story into the paper.

Most journalists who have reported on accidents and disasters for local papers have a story to tell about an emergency worker seeming to joke about a tragedy. Police, doctors and paramedics all have to devise ways of separating their work from family and other human relations, or they might not be able to carry on with the job. It is likely that, because on the whole journalists are keener to talk about their work, an apparent hardness of heart may be more noticeable.

It is the hard-bitten, cynical hacks who most often appear in plays and films as representing journalism, but on the other side of the coin (and there are plenty like this as well), are the idealists who genuinely want to 'make a difference'. They want to expose injustices, uncover corruption, or simply make their readers care more. It can be lonely and difficult work. Tom Bowyer, who spent years investigating the misdeeds of the *Mirror* tycoon Robert Maxwell, described the frustrations of compiling huge dossiers of facts and continually receiving injunctions preventing him from publishing what he knew to be the truth.

There is a debate raging at the moment in the field of war reporting about how much the reporting might affect the way events unfold. Wenlock Jakes in Evelyn Waugh's *Scoop* overslept in a train, ended up in the wrong country, filed extensively and fictionally about revolution going forward in a perfectly peaceable place, and ended up destabilising the country to such an extent that there really was a revolution.

Peace journalism is a fairly new and complicated subject, whose idealistic advocates want to use journalism to 'make a difference'. Its advocates say that all journalism is an intervention in a situation, that reporters should be aware of the effect of their reports, should seek to avoid stereotypes, try to report on conflict resolution rather than just on conflict, and in this way intervene to defuse a situation rather than worsen it.

The fictional Wenlock Jakes is an exaggeration, fortunately, but it is certainly the case that journalism, and in particular television, can have a huge effect on events. There are plenty of cases where the public in Britain has taken a great deal more interest in, and begun to do something about, a famine or disaster once the television cameras arrived. It might not look like it in some areas, but there are signs that journalism is becoming more responsible.

Probably the best-known campaigning journalist in Britain is Paul Foot, who has exposed corruption, scandal and injustice in his work for *The Mirror* and *Private Eye*. He wrote so regularly about the case of the men wrongfully imprisoned for the 1978 murder of the paperboy Carl Bridgewater that colleagues at *The Mirror* called him 'the man who thinks paperboys should be shot'.

Professor David Protess and his journalism students at the Medill School of Journalism at Northwestern University, Chicago, have had extraordinary successes with their campaigning. In joint work with the university's Department of Law, they succeeded in getting six innocent people freed, four of whom were on Death Row. In January 2003 the outgoing governor of Illinois, George

Ryan, emptied the state's Death Row of its 156 inhabitants when he commuted their sentences because, as he said, the journalism department's work had raised the spectre of errors of justice. Professor Protess and his team can certainly say they made a difference. Young would-be journalists are wary now of appearing too idealistic: they would rather say they simply want to get a job than change the world, but deep down most of them probably do hope to have the chance to do something which might 'make a difference'.

Idealistic or cynical, obsessed with football or with Elizabeth Hurley, there is room in journalism for many different types of people. Some of them need the attributes outlined above by the late *Sunday Times* correspondent Nicholas Tomalin. But not all have rat-like cunning, nor do they all have a plausible manner, and there are even some successful journalists with little or no literary ability. Tomalin would not be the first, when writing about the ideal person for a job like his own, to describe himself.

Care and devotion to accuracy, attention to detail, the ability to work in a team, the skill to encourage and get the best out of others, a determination simply to get things done on time, all these are qualities needed in different areas of newspapers and magazines.

A discussion about what journalists are like cannot ignore their reputation for hard drinking. The stories abound, and many of them are true. There was the senior agency man who sometimes made his way to the office in the morning from the police station at Snow Hill near Fleet Street after being arrested for drunkenness. A national newspaper desk editor was once so drunk that he fell downstairs, through a pair of doors, and disappeared into a hole in the ground when the plant at Wapping was still being built.

An editor's driver, who stopped in the Surrey countryside for a roadside call of nature, got back to the car to find his boss had woken up and wandered off into the night thinking he must be home. There were many hacks who, at their regular company medicals, were given serious talks by the doctor about their drinking habits being likely to lead to an early grave, when for the doctor's benefit they had halved the figure of their weekly intake. The Fleet Street pubs were legendary, too. There was the *Stab in the Back* (it did have another name, but no one used it) that had a door at the back as well as the front. The worry was that you would be quietly drinking at one end, and not see the senior editor enter at the other. The *Punch* still exists, where on rainy days the Fleet River, which runs underground below Ludgate Circus, seeps up and floods the men's lavatory in the basement, to the distress of the 'tired and emotional' hacks. The *Punch* has been much tidied up, as befits a pub surrounded now by merchant banks and corporate lawyers' offices. Much of this drinking has probably come to an end: journalists may have started paying attention to the stories they write about health issues, they work harder and have less time for drinking, and the dispersal of the national newspapers to the four corners of London has made for a much less convivial setting.

What qualities do you need to be a journalist?

This list, not exhaustive, is of some of the attributes I have seen in successful journalists:

Able to judge people:	everyone, but especially reporters and feature writers
Able to understand people:	everyone
Charming and friendly:	everyone, but especially reporters, feature writers and people on work experience, which means everyone when they start
Creative:	everyone
Cynical:	everyone, at least to enable them to judge the accuracy of a source
Determined:	everyone
Devious:	investigative reporters
Efficient:	everyone, but especially reporters and sub-editors
Full of ideas:	everyone, but especially specialist reporters, freelances, feature writers and editors
Fascinated by news:	everyone, but it might be news about international politics or it might be news about a celebrity romance or, heaven help us, another new diet

Hardworking:	everyone, if they want to get on
Idealistic:	everyone, at least when they start
Inquisitive:	everyone
Interested in language:	everyone, but especially sub-editors
Interested in people:	everyone, but especially reporters, feature writers
Methodical:	everyone, but especially sub-editors and freelances
Passionate about something:	everyone, but especially reporters, feature writers
Pernickety:	everyone, but especially sub-editors
Persistent:	everyone, but especially reporters
Persuasive:	reporters, freelances, commissioning editors
Possessed of good memory:	everyone, but especially sub-editors
Resilient:	everyone: journalists are not renowned for patting each other on the back. The fact that your story got into the paper or magazine at all is generally the only reward.
Tactful and thoughtful:	everyone, but particularly reporters, and particularly those specialising in human interest stories
Thick-skinned:	everyone: not only are there are often not many pats on the back, but there is plenty of flak. Getting a magazine or newspaper out at all is a very complicated team effort. If things go wrong it may be hard to apportion blame accurately, so it will probably be apportioned inaccurately
Well-read:	everyone, but especially sub-editors

If this list seems to cover everyone, from the extrovert joker to the almost painfully shy person who is a desktop publishing whiz, well that is right. It isn't true that every journalist is aggressive, opinionated, or full of him- or herself.

The world of journalism is so broad and diverse that there is a niche for everyone somewhere. The only real quality needed is determination, and a degree of self-belief. And if you are going to try to develop one of the above qualities more than any of the others, then think most about being charming and friendly. This will be essential in getting the first job. You can become obnoxious in your second or third jobs, and plenty of journalists do.

How does the job operate?

Lambert Le Roux (the press baron, just after buying the *Victory*): Are you a journalist?
Bill: Yes, actually.
Le Roux: You're hired.
Bill: No you can't fire me, I don't work for you....
Le Roux: No not *fired, hired...* I have many vacancies. Go and find any job you like.

Howard Brenton and David Hare, *Pravda*

Journalism has traditionally been regarded as a rather unsafe career, but as job security is no longer expected in so many other areas and as fewer people expect to have only one career in their working life, journalism is probably seen now as no more unsafe than plenty of other career choices.

Most journalists have staff jobs on their newspaper or magazine. But many thousands operate as freelances, in one of two ways. One is to get taken on to do shifts, especially on national newspapers, often as casual reporters, night news editors and subs. This is often the way young people operate at the start of their career, especially when they are trying to break into the nationals. The second way freelances work is to write news or features on a freelance basis, either approaching editors with ideas, or being approached by the editor who wants a particular subject covered. Many make a good living doing this, especially those who have developed a thorough specialism in one or two particular areas. Sometimes these are oddly esoteric: a freelance might cover the freight industry for one national paper, and archaeology for another. Most freelances of this type will have done some years of staff work before going freelance. It is hard to get started as a freelance without already having some contacts and a lot of expertise.

There is an increasing tendency for newspapers and magazines to offer short-term contracts, sometimes for a year, sometimes for a much shorter period. But this contract arrangement is now the norm in many other jobs too, from spin-doctoring to the church.

Contract and casual working adds to the general uncertainty of the job, but it does seem that casual shift workers who are good, and determined, do eventually end up with a staff job.

Working patterns

Many journalists have anti-social working hours. Big news agencies, such as the Press Association and Reuters, and websites such as bbc.co.uk work round the clock, with some staff coming in at 11 pm and working until 7 or 8 am. They will also, of course, work regularly at weekends.

Evening paper journalists generally have an early start, in some cases horrendously early. Some reporters and news editors at London's *Evening Standard* begin work at 5 am. There is also one overnight reporter who starts around midnight, spending the entire night reading through the national dailies looking for stories.

For morning newspaper reporters, the hours are similar to latish office workers' hours, perhaps starting around 10 am and finishing around 6 or 6.30 pm. But some reporters will stay late to incorporate more developments in their story for later editions. There will also always be late news desk staff, probably on the home, foreign and sports desks. These people will stay until early the following morning, monitoring the agencies, radio and television, ready to write up new stories that appear, or update existing stories with new developments. Reporters on national Sunday papers work notoriously long hours towards the end of the week, staying at the office until midnight or later on Fridays, which is when the finishing touches are put to many of the stories. Production people on morning papers will generally start work around lunchtime or during the afternoon, and go on until 10 pm, midnight or later. One or two journalists will be in the office of a morning paper until around 3 or 4 am, when the final edition goes to press. Those who work these hours generally work nine days in every fortnight, or even four days a week (with proportionately longer days), to compensate for the unsocial hours.

On magazines and weekly papers the hours are more like normal office hours, but journalists might expect to work late when the weekly or monthly deadline approaches. And of course if there is some particular event to be covered, and it happens in the evening or at the weekend, then the reporter will be there.

Salaries

Journalists are notoriously cagey about salaries. This may well be because there are often big differences in pay between people who do very similar jobs. I have known of a £10,000 difference in the pay of two first jobbers on the same national paper.

First jobs in journalism in the provinces are not well paid. Indeed, many local papers want 18-year-old school leavers who can live at home, because their pay would not cover the rent of a flat. Pay on a local paper might start at between £10,000 and £12,000 but would rise slowly but surely, so that a qualified reporter at 21 would earn about £15,000–£17,000. There are some awful cases of well-known and profitable regional newspaper groups paying as little as £8,000. Not surprisingly, the National Union of Journalists is campaigning about this, and has instituted a 'Scrooge of the Year' award for the regional paper company that pays worst. The union is also campaigning against university top-up fees because, with students already in debt, they will have great difficulty in paying off any more on the low salaries paid on local papers. According to the union, graduates across every type of career earn an average of £20,000 after a year in their first job. There is no doubt that local paper trainees do not generally earn anywhere near that.

A news editor on a weekly would earn something between £21,000 and £25,000, and a bit more in London or the south east.

A trainee with a degree and perhaps with a postgraduate qualification could expect to start at £14,000 to £16,000 on a regional paper or an agency, or a couple of thousand more starting as a trainee on a national.

A qualified young reporter on a regional paper would earn around £22,000 to £24,000.

Pay on magazines is generally slightly higher, and a first job on a business to business (B2B) magazine such as the *Grocer* or *Nursing Times* would pay about £16,000 to £18,000, and this salary would rise commensurately. The financial newsletters and the international agencies pay considerably better salaries to young recruits.

There is a huge discrepancy between jobs in what is still known as Fleet Street (although almost no journalists now work there) and jobs in the provinces. A senior reporter or sub-editor on a national would earn between £35,000 and £50,000, with a deputy section head or specialist earning at the top of that range or higher.

Writers whose bylines become well known as interviewers, reviewers or columnists can command very substantial fees. There are reports that Paul Dacre, editor-in-chief of the *Daily Mail*, earns £850,000. Maybe, like the L'Oreal girl in the advertisement, he is worth it.

On the whole, pay on the tabloids seems to be slightly higher than on broadsheet papers, especially for sub-editors, whose skills at writing snappy headlines and cutting copy carefully are highly prized.

Not so long ago, a trainee with a postgraduate diploma from City University went to an agency (not a very well-respected one) on a salary of £7,000 a year. The same year another went to the financial agency Bloomberg for £35,000 a year. Perhaps the most that can be said about starting salaries in journalism is that they will be somewhere between those two figures.

2

newspapers

- *The newspaper industry*
- *The news team*
- *The production team*
- *The features team*
- *Stand-alone sections*
- *The senior editorial team*

> '"We think it a very promising little war. A microcosm, as you might say, of world drama. We propose to give it fullest publicity. The workings of a great newspaper," said Lord Copper, feeling at last thoroughly Rotarian, "are of a complexity which the public seldom appreciates. The citizen little realizes the vast machinery put into motion for him in exchange for his morning penny."
> ("O God," said Lady Metroland, faintly but audibly.)'
>
> Evelyn Waugh, *Scoop*

Britain is extremely well served with newspapers, and probably has the biggest selection of genuinely national newspapers in the world. There are ten national dailies ranging from *The Star* to the *Financial Times*, and 11 national Sundays. In addition, there are papers aimed exclusively at Scotland, Northern Ireland and Wales, which are variously described as regional or national, depending on where you are standing.

There are about 100 regional dailies (evening and morning), though in general, the circulation of regional mornings is low and falling, so this figure may change. Then there are about 500 paid-for local weekly papers, and about 600 free local papers.

The newspaper industry

British national newspapers are generally divided into three categories. The broadsheets: *The Daily Telegraph, The Times, The Guardian,* the *Financial Times* and *The Independent,* which are seen as more 'serious' than the tabloids; the middle market tabloids – the *Daily Mail* and the *Express;* and the 'red-tops', meaning the racy tabloids, the *Mirror,* the *Sun* and the *Daily Star.* It seems likely that in spite of their 'compact' editions, the term broadsheet will stick for the moment.

The regional dailies are generally centred on large urban areas, with people in very rural places possibly not feeling very well served by any regional daily. Many areas are covered by more than one weekly local paper, and more than one 'free sheet'. These free newspapers, financed entirely by advertising, are generally delivered through every letterbox in their circulation area. Sometimes they may also be picked up in shops and stations. They are often owned by the same big firms which own many of the paid-for weeklies, and close inspection may reveal that the staff and the stories are the same or similar.

A new arrival in the past decade has been the daily *Metro* newspapers. These are given out or can be picked up at stations in big cities in the mornings. They, too, are financed entirely by advertising, generally of jobs, property and cars. The first was the London *Metro* and others quickly followed elsewhere. There were battles between rival firms which all started similar projects in several big cities in the past few years. Associated Newspapers now has *Metros* in several major cities, including London, Birmingham, Manchester and Glasgow; in some cases in partnership with local groups.

Over the past 20 years or more, newspapers of all types have expanded enormously in size, and the Saturday and Sunday nationals particularly are constantly bringing out new sections, covering everything from gardening to motoring to personal finance. This means there are more jobs in these areas. In 2003 *The Times* might have about 20 pages of home and foreign news every day, plus perhaps another ten on sport. In 1967, as recorded in John Grigg's history of the paper, it had five pages a day. In the 1960s these pages would have had more words on them than nowadays: the headlines and pictures would have been smaller and there would have been smaller and fewer advertisements, but the fact is that there are far more words in the papers now than there used to be. This huge difference in the volume of words is the defence cited by broadsheet editors when accused of 'dumbing down' their papers. Yes, they say, we do cover Mick Jagger's divorce, but we still cover all the other (more important) stuff as well. This does not always convince the 'Disgusteds of Tunbridge Wells', however. Either way, it has meant more jobs, and more young people getting on to nationals probably rather earlier in their careers than they used to do 30 or 40 years ago. Including casuals and people on short-term contracts, *The Times* now has a staff of 650–700 journalists, up by about 250–300 on the figure ten years ago.

Local papers, which have also increased their pagination over this period, seem in general to have done so by making sure the journalists work harder and faster: staff numbers on local papers have shrunk in some places over the past 20 to 25 years. And local papers have proportionately fewer trainees than they did a couple of generations ago. Then it was common for a local newspaper to have a chief reporter, one other qualified reporter and perhaps half a dozen trainees. Quite a few of these papers now have a smaller staff, but with perhaps three or four experienced journalists, and only one or two trainees.

This chapter deals with the jobs involved in writing and editing the words in newspapers. Later chapters deal with graphics, pictures and online journalism.

The news team

These are the general reporters, specialists and news editors who between them write the words that appear in the news sections of the paper.

General news reporters

Most of those starting in journalism on local and regional newspapers do so as news reporters, covering anything and everything that happens. A general reporter on a local paper will write stories about crime, accidents, council shake-ups, hospitals and factories opening or closing, planning decisions, golden weddings, new vicars, the birth of a child to a local celebrity – the list is endless. On a national, the stories might be similar, but they would simply be bigger stories. A former student, in one week as a general reporter at the Press Association, spent one day door-stepping the home of Paula Yates on the day she heard of the death in Australia of her lover Michael Hutchence; the next she was at a major banquet where the speaker was Gordon Brown; the next she was meeting some British tourists at Heathrow as they returned, some injured, after being involved in a bus crash on holiday; and on the fourth she was at a service to mark the Queen's Golden Wedding. So she can't have been short of dinner-party conversation that week.

Usually, general reporters cover stories as assigned by a news editor. There are broadly three ways the reporter collects the news: by going to events, by responding to material that the paper receives, and by following up contacts and leads. Reporters go to courts, council and other meetings, police and other press conferences, demonstrations, planning inquiries, openings of supermarkets, galleries or new wine bars. They may also make regular calls, for example to fire stations and the police.

Information is sent in to the newspaper's office in the form of press releases, by the council, local health authority, or a local business. Many individuals contact local papers too, and these might range from a daughter telling the paper about her parents' golden wedding to someone complaining about some perceived injustice. General reporters will check all these things out for possible stories. They will also build up personal contacts, such as with a councillor, an individual who regularly campaigns on development issues, someone involved in education, and so on. Reporters also monitor other news outlets, such as rival papers and local radio stations, to make sure they haven't missed any stories. More stories are found by following up earlier reports – such as visiting an estate where a spate of muggings took place last week and reporting on residents calling for closed circuit TV security systems. Good reporters also bring in their own **off-diary** stories: they notice that a recently opened café has just closed, they see a postcard ad for an all-female emergency plumbing firm, or notice that a new shop has opened which sells rubber knickers and handcuffs, and follow these up.

It is unlikely that papers would have the resources to send reporters out simply on an off-diary hunt. But a good paper would at least allow time to meet contacts and certainly reporters would be expected to spend some leisure time in the area. Good reporters pick up off-diary stories in the pub, or by being observant on their way to work. Off-diary work brings in 'bottom-up' stories rather than the 'top-down' stories reporters generally get by talking to council leaders, police and the like. The theory is that off-diary stories are about ordinary people rather than leaders. But the snag, of course, with such material is that it can at worst turn into a catalogue of whingeing about the council, health authority, or police.

In all areas of journalism far more interviewing is done on the phone than was the case a generation ago. It is quicker to talk to people on the phone, and by doing that reporters get more stories written each day. But there is a corresponding lack of the deep local knowledge that reporters had some years ago.

Specialist reporters

Big regionals and nationals will have a team of specialist reporters. On small local papers too, reporters will often be assigned to cover some of the major areas – crime, education, the council – although they will probably cover other stories as well.

On nationals, up to six or so reporters will cover politics and parliament, and there will be others writing political columns and features. There might be two covering education and two more covering health, and these reporters will also contribute to weekly education and health features sections. The broadsheet nationals will have big teams covering sport and business and finance. There will be specialists covering many other areas including crime, health, religion, transport, the media, science, technology and so on.

Specialist areas come and go according to what is currently newsworthy, and perhaps a little according to the editor's special interests. In the 1970s *The Times* had three reporters covering trade union affairs: a labour editor and two labour reporters. Such is the lack of news about trade unions, or their lack of power, or a lack of interest in their affairs, that there is no specialist at *The Times* covering that area now. On the other hand, many papers now have environment and possibly development correspondents as these subjects are seen to have grown in importance.

Specialist reporters are expected to know about and cover news events in their areas, to have enough knowledge to report complicated issues accurately and to build up contacts they can interview to fill out their stories. They are expected to watch their beat closely so they can spot potential stories that they would hope to report as **exclusives** – before rival newspapers find the same story. This is seen as extremely important on the national Sunday papers, where reporters spend most of their time 'working up' stories which they hope no other paper, most especially the other Saturday papers, will find. This has led to a very different kind of story appearing in Sunday papers because of the pressure to get something different from rivals. Some Sunday journalists are happy with the word **infotainment**, which has come to mean slightly gossipy or speculative stories that do not add enormously to the sum of human knowledge. Others are perhaps less impressed with the way news stories are worked up. There are many reports of daily national newspaper reporters spending regular Sunday-for-Monday shifts following up these speculative stories which were in the Sundays, and finding that they do not always, in the journalistic phrase, 'stand up'.

Some specialist reporters cover the same area for many years, acquiring a very deep knowledge of the subject and the people involved. They may write spin-off books: crime reporters sometimes write quick books about a particularly newsworthy crime, an education correspondent might write education guides, a sports reporter might ghost a sporting personality's autobiography. These specialists might also pop up as TV pundits. Some papers like to move specialists around from time to time to prevent them from 'going native': there have been plenty of cases where reporters end up having more allegiance to their sources than to their employer.

News Editor
The news editor is the 'line manager' to all the reporters. A national newspaper will have four or five news editors, all working as a team on the **newsdesk**. For someone who has never seen it, the scene on a big paper's newsdesk can seem like pandemonium, especially at a busy time on a busy news day. Many phones ring constantly, there is noise from several televisions and radios, as well as people running around and discussing stories, sometimes noisily.

The news editors monitor other news sources, including news agencies, rival papers, TV and radio broadcasts. They check what the specialists plan to cover, discuss angles and likely development. They commission reporters to cover as many stories as possible and constantly monitor news sources to try to make sure nothing important is missed. A major part of the news editor's role is to produce a **news list** which is discussed at the **conference**. On a national paper the first of these will be held in the middle of the morning. At this point some stories may be rejected by the editor, who may want other possible stories investigated. The news editor will also liaise with the picture desk to try to ensure that there will be pictures to go with major stories.

News editors will monitor the progress of stories, check that reporters are going to be able to file their copy in time for the edition, and ensure that the stories match up to what was offered at the morning conference. They read through the stories as they are written, suggesting other points that might be covered, checking that two or three related stories form a coherent **package**. Researchers might be commissioned to go through the database to produce **sidebars**, such as chronologies of recent related events, or '10 things you didn't know about XXX', to go with the news stories.

Two or three **news desk secretaries** will also work on the desk, fielding phone calls, checking where reporters are, sorting out expenses, travel and accommodation. They are highly efficient, often somewhat intimidating, people.

The task of the news editors and reporting team is to provide enough, or rather more than enough, **copy** to fill the paper. On national newspapers many stories do not make it into the paper. It is not unknown for established reporters on some nationals to find that, at the end of a week of solid writing, only one of their stories has appeared in the paper. The production team will want to have considerably more copy than they need, to give them plenty of leeway to cut stories down or discard them if there is not quite the right slot for them in the paper. This is one of the many reasons that the design of national newspapers is generally so much slicker than that of local papers. It also accounts for the fact that if you read several national newspapers on the same day, even papers which could be said to be in the same market, such as *The Guardian* and *The Independent*, for example, you will find some seemingly important stories in one paper but not the other. Papers make no attempt to tell their readers all the major events that happened yesterday, they seek only to record the things that happened yesterday in which they believe their readers will be interested. At its worst, this means running only certain stories on some issues which will confirm what the news editors believe to be their readers' world view. The debate over asylum seekers is the current best/worst example of this.

Whatever use they make of this power, the fact is that a national newspaper production team has the luxury of enough material to fill or cut into a specific design. On a small local paper the production team will probably have to use almost everything the newsdesk provides, which makes generally for a much bittier and less attractive design.

On national newspapers there will also be a **foreign newsdesk**, with **foreign news editors** working with correspondents abroad, and a small team in London covering the foreign office and diplomatic affairs in London, as well as providing background stories and London angles to foreign events. The foreign desk will liaise with staff reporters abroad, if there are any, and generally a large number of **stringers** – freelances in different parts of the world who may or may not have a contract with the paper to cover events where they live. Some may be paid a retainer that pays part of their rent (their home will be their office) and telephone calls, while they get extra money for pieces which get into the paper. Others may earn more for what they write, but very little in the way of a retainer. Certainly the retainer will include a clause preventing them from writing for a rival publication, although this doesn't always stop them. The contracts which stringers manage to negotiate are often mysterious and hard to pin down. Foreign editors are very reluctant to reveal what deals have been agreed, which suggests that different individuals strike deals which are not necessarily comparable with each other.

It is sad but true that most British newspapers, apart from the ever-expanding *Financial Times*, now have very few foreign correspondents. They rely on local stringers and the major international agencies such as Reuters. If a story is big enough they will send a reporter from London to cover it, although the reported 500 journalists who covered David Beckham's arrival to play for Real Madrid in 2003 seem like overkill. Most papers rely on agencies for coverage of even major events in the political life of other countries. The person who wants to be a journalist in order to travel around the world at someone else's expense would be better off becoming an air hostess.

The production team

'...the first view of *The Times* office in London. In the Foreign Editorial Room a sub-editor was translating a passage of Plato's *Phaedo* into Chinese, for a bet. Another sub-editor had declared it could not be done without losing a certain nuance of the original. He was dictating the Greek passage aloud from memory.'

Claud Cockburn, *I Claud*

UP YOURS DELORS

Front page headline, *The Sun*

When the stories have all been written, or at least the first versions produced, they move within the newspaper's computer system into a production basket or queue. The focus of the operation then becomes the responsibility, on a national paper, of the **night editor**, the **back bench** and the **sub-editors**, or **subs**.

At another news conference, often known as, for example, 'the four o'clock', the editor and deputy editor, with the night editor and team, will have decided which stories will go on the front, which others will make **page leads**, and on which pages. As the stories come in, the night editor, his or her assistants and probably a home and foreign chief sub, will have designed and made the pages ready, using sophisticated desk-top publishing software.

Big nationals often have their own specially designed or adapted system. Smaller papers will probably use off-the-peg design software such as QuarkXPress or Adobe InDesign. Increasingly, a separate **design team** of people whose background is graphic design rather than editing will have a role in preparing the pages. These are designed using templates that come from the advertising department, showing where adverts have been sold. The back bench and design team will work to a **flat plan**, a page or pages showing thumbnail-sized numbered pairs of boxes corresponding to each spread of the paper. As the senior editorial team work out which main stories are going where, the squares are filled in with a phrase or two to convey each story. With the amount of material in newspapers today, a great deal of care needs to be taken to make sure related stories are placed together, that two versions of the same story do not appear (easily done), or that a story about famine does not appear next to an advert for a supermarket's delicious new range of food.

Stories are positioned extremely carefully within the paper. The left-hand, even-numbered pages are regarded as slightly less important, and slightly weaker stories and pictures are placed there. The strongest, liveliest stories and the best pictures go on the odd-numbered pages, and the better the story, the nearer the front it goes. In all papers, page three is regarded as the second most important news page after the front, and much thought goes into selecting a lively, often human interest story or package of stories for this slot. Many years ago *The Sun* decided what would be best for this page, and their consistency in this has led to an entirely new dictionary definition of the phrase 'page three'.

Sub-editors

As the production deadlines approach, stories are allocated places on each page, and instructions showing where they are to go are added to their computer headers. The **sub-editors** then edit each story.

Subs work at a configuration of desks and computers known as a 'subs' table'. The sub-editing equivalent of general reporters are **down-table subs**. Their job is to check each story, make sure it reads well, and make sure there are no **holes**, journalists' jargon for a burning but unanswered question likely to arise in the mind of the reader. Subs check as many facts as they can, consider whether the story might be libellous, and satisfy themselves that it is not (or refer it to the in-house lawyers if the reporter or news editor has not already done so). At the same time they cut the story to exactly the length to fill the gap in the page to which it has been allocated. Modern desk top publishing programs are known as 'wysiwyg systems', meaning 'What You See Is What You Get', so subs can cut the story to precisely the right length because they are working on a computer version of the exact page. Instructions for the size and typeface of the headline will have been added, so the sub is also able to write a headline. Writing good snappy headlines, of which a *Sun* classic appears above, is one of the subs' most important tasks. It takes an innate flair and a great deal of practice. Subbing on tabloids, where all the stories are so much shorter than on broadsheets, is highly skilled, and tabloid subs on average earn slightly more than those on broadsheets. It is a common misapprehension that one might start on a tabloid and move to a broadsheet, that working on a tabloid is somehow easier. In fact the reverse is probably the case.

The sub is the first 'new reader' to look at the story. The news editor knew all about it when reading it, after discussing it with the reporter during the day. The reporter, who knows the whole issue inside out, may have left out some important point which is obvious to her, but would not be to a general reader. But the sub is the first person who looks at the story as the paper's readers will. This makes it easier to spot if, for example, a vital issue is left unexplained.

The journalistic tradition is that reporters hate subs, because they cut and alter their exquisite prose, removing a brilliant turn of phrase which the reporter slaved over (but which the sub thought was naff). A common reporters' joke goes something like this: 'Subbing means removing the first and last paragraph, and taking out all the jokes'. The subs, on the other hand, despise the reporters because they don't understand the apostrophe rules, or they couldn't even spell the name of the cabinet minister correctly, or they didn't know that it was Newcastle-UPON-Tyne, and so on. In fact, compared to a couple of decades ago, the two sides now probably see themselves as less in opposition to each other than they once did. This may be because there is a slightly freer movement between the two jobs than there used to be.

Matthew Parris, a columnist on *The Times* and a broadcaster, wrote a generous tribute in the preface to his recent book *Chance Witness*: 'Columnists love to moan about subs but I must speak for myself: time and again the subs have saved me from errors in my journalism, some of them real howlers. They have cut and left no scars. They have spotted mistakes I had no right to hope anyone would check, and tactfully hinted when the argument was not clear. Editing cannot always be felicitous nor can every headline hit the target, but I decided early that these people were much, much better at it than me and I would leave them to it. I've never regretted that approach.'

The back bench
The subbing team reports to the chief sub, and ultimately, on a morning paper, to the night editor, who is responsible for the entire production operation. Hierarchies will vary on newspapers but in general there will be a **back bench**, presided over by the night editor; the editor and/or deputy editor may also sit there during the late afternoon or early evening. At Westminster, back bench MPs have little or no power or say in major political decisions, but the back bench on a newspaper is where all the main decisions are taken about the front page lead, or **splash**, the choice of front page picture, and so on.

Other senior members of this team include **copytasters**, whose responsibility it is to read all the stories that come in (from reporters, agencies and stringers), check that each one chosen for publication is worthy of its place, and that nothing better has been missed. In the subbing operation the buck stops with the **revise sub-editors**, who go through all the stories after they have been subbed, to give them yet another check over. Another senior sub, possibly an assistant night editor, will generally edit the lead story, and is sometimes known as the **splash sub**.

On tabloid papers some of these people and others occupy a **middle bench**. In fact on a tabloid the back bench and middle bench probably include up to 20 journalists. The traditional route into subbing is via reporting, and most subs start their careers on a local paper, move into subbing at that point, and either progress through the ranks there, or move to a national subs' table. But the difficulty of recruiting subs means that some national and regional papers are starting training schemes to nurture new young subs, and recently the *Daily Mail* arranged a much-hyped subbing course through the Press Association.

On a small local paper the set-up will be the same as outlined above, but with all the tasks shared between a much smaller number of people. There won't be a copytaster because all the material gets into the paper anyway, and the editor will probably design the front page and revise as much copy as possible.

Weeklies often have one or two reporter/subs, who research and write stories early in the week, and edit and design pages on the day the paper goes to press.

The features team

On local papers reporters usually write features in between their news writing commitments, and these will be edited and designed into pages by the editor or deputy editor. Big regionals and nationals, however, have an increasing demand for features of all kinds, as papers become ever larger, so these papers have separate features operations. The features department will be similar to the news one, with a writing team providing the stories and a production team, probably led by a chief features sub, designing and producing the pages. Sometimes it is hard, on a paper like the *Daily Mail* for instance, to see exactly which things might have originated on the features desk. All the papers now use a great many **soft** stories (as opposed to **hard** news about crime, political developments, or international strife) and these soft, or sometimes **fluffy** news stories often look very feature-like. They might be 'news' about anything, from what Cherie Blair has been wearing to a random little survey which shows that parents are increasingly helping their grown-up children with house purchase. The stories which started as features rather than news might look quite similar, but would probably have more pictures and more comment. A health story about some new figures relating to a particular form of cancer, perhaps, might appear on the news pages as a fairly brief item, but might resurface on the features pages a week or two later, with interviews with a consultant and someone who has started a support group, and a couple of case studies about families affected by this disease.

Feature writers

National newspapers will have a small team, maybe only about half a dozen, permanent feature writers. Many of them will also write for other areas of the paper, such as a **colour** piece about some political or royal event. Other specialists on the paper will probably write pieces about their areas of expertise, and every paper has a large pool of freelances who write with varying regularity. Feature writing is traditionally the province of experienced journalists, as it is obviously not an easy task to conduct interviews and structure a

2,000-word piece about, say, shortcomings in a council social services department. However, with the proliferation of small items about make-up, what is the best packet of crisps on the market, where to find a converted barn for sale, and so on, there is plenty of scope for less experienced people, if they can get a foot in the door. Any good feature writer or features editor will have a permanent list of possible ideas somewhere, in fact in two places, both in the Palm Pilot and jotted in the back of a conventional diary. This list gets added to, refined, changed slightly as a new angle becomes possible, and so on. Unfortunately, ideas must be crossed off from time to time when a rival paper runs exactly the same story. But even that can reappear on the list in a few weeks' time, when most people might have forgotten it again.

Feature researchers

This is a fairly junior job, often done by a recent graduate, but is a good way into journalism. The researcher may do anything, from finding several different kinds of garden lighting to tracking down converted windmills or people to be interviewed about something. The features editor may want to know whether a particular idea will, in the journalistic phrase, **stand up**. So the researcher might find himself investigating the background about the fridge mountain one day, for example, and the increase in people setting themselves up as animal psychologists the next. On tabloids the ideas may sometimes be considerably saucier, although it is often a freelance feature writer rather than a researcher who will be trying to find six women (all good-looking, of course) who have had sex with their best friend's partner but still remained friends, AND are prepared to be interviewed and photographed.

Commissioning editors

These people liaise with freelances and those on specific contracts, talking about ideas, and finding out how work is progressing. Some can be quite senior jobs, but it is possible to get a first job as a junior commissioning editor. In the early stages this may be rather like a news desk secretary's job: tracking people down, asking if they would like to write something, and generally keeping tabs on what is being done and by whom. It is possible to progress from there to a more senior decision-making role, or to a writing role.

Features editor

On nationals the features editor may be responsible for a separate section, such as *The Guardian's* G2, or for a large number of features pages in the main paper. A feature could be anything from an item in a gossip column about an 'IT-girl', to a serious piece about restructuring the health service. There have traditionally been, and are still, a greater proportion of women working in features departments than in other areas of the paper. This might be because the hours are generally more flexible, or because traditionally there have always been more features aimed at women (it is only very recently that papers began to feature men's fashion at all). Or it might be that women are simply better at securing and doing interviews, at getting the human side of a story that makes for a successful feature.

The features editor has to have plenty of ideas, know what angles might work and who might cover them, and have the ability to supervise the whole operation. A good features editor thinks of ideas before the rivals think of them, spots trends before the competition, and finds interesting people to be interviewed or to write pieces.

After reading her own paper, and those of the main rivals, the features editor's day will probably start with a features conference involving most or all of the team, and possibly the editor or deputy editor of the paper, to go through the previous day's paper, discuss events in the news and bounce ideas off each other. A rough list of ideas to be followed up will be prepared, and the team will also monitor progress on longer-term features on which writers are already working.

There is also constant pressure to keep ahead of rival newspapers. So on national papers there are always new plans in the pipeline, new sections, new columns, redesigns of existing sections, and so on. Rarely, it seems, do the top brass on nationals leave anything alone for very long.

Celebrity interviewers

Most features sections also have at least one celebrity interviewer. The good ones generally do an enormous amount of research before interviewing someone, and papers seem happy to send some of them halfway round the world to conduct one interview.

Some celebrity interviewers conduct and write an interview every week, others prefer or need to spend more time on research (as might well be the case with a subject who is a prolific author, for example) and so they do one interview every couple of weeks or less. A good celebrity interviewer reads all the cuttings of previous interviews with the subject, possibly talks to friends, colleagues or rivals of the subject, and then comes up with something new, rather than simply going over old ground. Nowhere is the saying 'more means worse' more true than with the proliferation of celebrity interviewers, many of whom fail to provide a particularly new insight into the subject's character or work at all. Lynn Barber is still the queen of this genre and her interviews always give a new insight into the subject. As with other feature writers, some of these interviewers, rather than having staff jobs, are on a contract to produce a certain number of pieces a year.

Columnists

'Sometimes, when he was really worried about what to write about next, he would sit at dinnertime, his eyes darting desperately around the room. Was there a column in the salt and pepper shakers? In the paper napkins? In the Cuisinart food processor?'

Nora Ephron, *Heartburn*, the narrator writing about Mark, her main character's Washington columnist husband

There has been a huge increase in the number of first person columns in newspapers. Some are written by people who got the contract because they were already celebrities of sorts (it is still hard to believe that *The Guardian* took on a disgraced *Conservative* minister, David Mellor, as a columnist). Others, such as Richard Littlejohn on *The Sun* and Lynda Lee Potter of *The Mail*, have become celebrities because of their columns. These columns vary greatly. Some, known as **me columns**, often involve milking the columnist's own family: 'Here's some interesting things my two-year old/granny/husband/teenage daughter said last week.' Me columns might also be about more general domestic material: 'Here's some stuff about a recent PTA meeting/my new cooker/my holiday.' Many have become so inconsequential that they are easily parodied – the brilliant Polly Filler in *Private Eye* is so funny because she is practically indisting-uishable from all too many award-winning columnists.

The most successful me columns are by those to whom dramatic things are happening, <u>and</u> who can write very well. The pairing of Taki Theodoracopoulos writing *High Life*, and Jeffrey Bernard writing *Low Life* in *The Spectator* was legendary. Then there have been several columns charting the columnists' own fatal illnesses, including Oscar Moore who wrote with great courage and humour in *The Guardian* until his death from AIDS in 1996 and, most famous of all, John Diamond charting in *The Times* his impending death from cancer in 2001. Jeffrey Bernard also came into this category in the end, as he became more and more ill from diabetes until he died in 1997. These last three columnists' writings were all made into plays, with *Jeffrey Bernard is Unwell* becoming a major West End hit. The title is the line used in *The Spectator* when he was too drunk or too ill to write his column. Unsurprisingly, 'first person death columns' have gone out of fashion at the moment, as most things do sooner or later in journalism.

Other columns are known in the trade as **think-pieces**, **rants** or **why-oh-why** columns: 'Why oh why doesn't Tony Blair/the Royal Opera House/Islington Social Services do such and such?' Some why-oh-why columnists have become so expert at it that they can rant in one direction for a newspaper at the beginning of the week, and in the opposite direction in a news magazine at the end of the week. It is unlikely, but not unknown, for fairly new recruits to get into this, although they usually do so by catching the editor's eye in some other way. Craig Brown's brilliant parodies of these columns, under the fictional byline of Bel Littlejohn, appeared in *The Guardian* for so long that the character took on a life of her own. Greatly to the glee of those who got the joke, she had a regular postbag of letters, and was occasionally invited to speak somewhere.

A new, and perhaps slightly unwelcome, type of column is the fictional one. It began, or certainly took off, with a column called *Bad Housekeeping* in *The Guardian* a few years ago. The character, Dulcie Domum, wrote about her tedious husband, her irritating children, her unfinished novel and the young plumber with whom she embarked on an affair. It all got very crazy and far-fetched in the end. The best known of these fictions of course is Bridget Jones, who started life as a spoof column in *The Independent*.

The trouble with these columns is that they may be partly responsible for creating an atmosphere in which some of the dozens of young columnists around think they can make up a few things to bring a bit more excitement into their writings. And I fear plenty of them do. It is but a short step from there to fabricating a few interviews to strengthen a feature. Newspapers, in my view, should be about things that actually happened. Things that don't belong in novels.

Leaders, comment and letters sections

'Harry (the Editor): Hitler worked out very well for the *Bystander*. Because we saw him coming. It enhanced our reputation. not that it wasn't a pretty close thing. I caught this phrase "Mr Hitler is refreshingly dynamic". Thought oh dear, not very wise. Changed it to 'unnecessarily dynamic'.'

Howard Brenton and David Hare, *Pravda*

All papers have leaders, that is, columns which are not bylined and are therefore intended to represent the paper's stance on the issues of the day. Much thought is given to these on every paper, especially in times of crisis such as the Iraq war or at election time, when the papers and their proprietors believe, rightly or wrongly, that they may actually influence people's voting decisions. It is impossible to pin down whether newspapers do have the influence they claim. On the day of the general election in 1992, *The Sun's* front page declared, with a picture of Neil Kinnock's head as a light bulb: 'If Labour wins today will the last person to leave Britain please turn out the lights.' The next day, after Labour had been unexpectedly defeated, the paper's front page claimed 'It was the Sun Wot Won it'. But it is impossible to work out whether people voted the way they did because they were influenced by their paper, or whether it was a case of the paper wisely telling its readers to do exactly what it realised they were likely to do anyway. On a broadsheet national the editor may write some leaders, but even if he doesn't he will take a close interest in them and probably chair a leader conference to agree the line to be taken with the several people who are ready to write the two or three leaders needed every day. The same people probably also write elsewhere in the paper, either bylined columns of their more personal views, or commentaries on particular areas such as politics or the economy. The very short leaders in red-top tabloids are generally written by a senior political commentator, or sometimes by an assistant editor or other senior journalist. Local and regional paper editors often write their own leaders.

Bylined comment pieces, often on national or international politics, appear on the comment, or **op-ed** page, so called because it is generally opposite the editorial page. The columnists, some perhaps staff but many freelance, with some sub-editors, all come under the wing of the comment editor, and on a broadsheet national this makes up a separate department. As well as assigning leader writers, the comment editor will discuss what is going on the op-ed page and commission and liaise with freelance columnists, many of whom will have a regular slot on a particular day of the week. On the op-ed page the writers are free to disagree, and they often do, with the line taken in the leaders.

All newspapers have letters pages, although on local papers these can look suspiciously as though they are a cheap way to fill a couple of pages. Every local councillor writes in regularly setting out their own achievements or their opponents' shortcomings. These must be among the least-read sections of the papers. Tabloids tend to use their pages for letters with jokey anecdotes, maybe a witty or interesting riposte to a columnist, or heart-warming family stories. On most regional papers, selecting the letters and designing the page will fall to a sub or news editor. On nationals there will be a separate team led by a senior journalist. The *Times* letters page is a national institution and many leaders in the worlds of the arts, religion, charities or other pressure groups view it as an important forum in which to air their views. The page has a team of four journalists who read every letter and email – an average of almost 500 a day. They make a shortlist for possible publication and gradually refine that list during the day. *The Times* has a rule that it won't carry letters that have been sent to any other paper as well, and indeed there are still plenty of people out there who harbour an ambition to get a letter into the paper. The writer of each letter chosen for publication gets a phone call to check that he or she actually exists, and wrote the letter that has come in. The team may also want to make editing changes to the letter, and all these have to be agreed with the writer. The letters editor keeps a very close eye on what is in the news, and makes sure that every letter earns its place on the page, either by adding to the national debate on an issue or simply by being clever or witty.

Comment and letters sections are unlikely to be fruitful areas for a young person starting out in journalism. The comment section may, however, provide a home for someone who is either already known in some other area, or has some expertise in, say, politics or the academic world. Leo McKinstry, a former Labour councillor in Islington and Labour political researcher, suddenly decided the Labour Party and its politics were not for him. He left the council and his job, wrote a piece for the *Daily Mail* about his sudden decision, and has been a journalist ever since. At one stage he had a regular page in the *Daily Mail* called 'Around the Clown Councils' detailing some of the more way-out decisions taken by Labour councils around the country. But his success is rare, and trying to emulate it would not make a very viable career plan for many people.

Obituaries

'"We'd be very grateful if you hear that anyone is (cough) not, um, well, if you let us know, so that we can, um, prepare." I did not like the way he measured my pallor; I was suffering from a lingering cold.'

Harold Evans, *Good Times, Bad Times* describing meeting the obituaries editor, Colin Watson, when Evans took over the editorship of *The Times*

The activities of the **obits** department are generally a source of great wonder to anyone not experienced in the newspaper world. Most national papers will have big obituaries departments, perhaps three or four full-time journalists, with large numbers of freelances contributing pieces. They will have several hundred obituaries ready to go straight into the paper if the subject suddenly dies. What can cause astonishment to the casual observer is that the subjects of these profiles are in some cases quite young and in generally good health. But of course if the team does hear that someone is in poor health they will most definitely call up their obit and dust it off. As well as choosing and giving the final edit to obituaries for the day's paper, the team spends its time commissioning new ones. They also update the existing obituaries, adding new facts as the subject either takes on a different political role, leaves his wife, is fired, or goes to jail. For major figures there will be special sections all ready to go, with headlines and pictures. The most obvious example, of course, was the Queen Mother as she neared the end of her life, when all the papers were ready with special sections filled with stories, sidebars and pictures of her at every age.

Writing obituaries can be quite a lucrative area for a freelance who knows lots of figures in, say, the world of arts or sport. Often a fairly good friend or colleague of the subject is asked to write their obituary. Traditionally there were no bylines on obituaries: the whole thing was so carefully prepared and thought about that the paper was happy to publish the obituary as its own considered view. But when *The Independent* was launched it was decided that the author's name would be included and, soon after, *The Guardian* copied this practice. This does alter the emphasis somewhat – the paper is not saying 'Here is our definitive summary of this person's life,' but instead it is saying 'Here is what X thinks about Y' which may devalue it slightly. The electronic storage of obituaries in newspapers is made very secure: there is a tradition that no one should be able to read their own obituary, and stories abound of major figures wanting to see theirs. Apparently Winston Churchill tried, but failed, to get a glimpse of the obituary that *The Times* had prepared of him.

Arts and books

These are big sections, especially on broadsheets, each with an editor, several staff writers, a secretary, and perhaps a dedicated subbing team. Much of the material will be contributed: most reviewers, for example, will be freelances contracted to write a certain number of reviews and/or features each year.

As well as reviews, arts sections carry interviews and features about forthcoming plays or films, columns of recommendations and cut-down reviews of films and plays that have already opened. This is not a very likely area for a first job, because it would be hard to convince the editor you are an expert (even if you are), and because in some areas, television reviewing for instance, the papers want an experienced and very lively writer, rather than an expert. However, would-be journalists do get jobs on these desks, sometimes in a semi-secretarial role, and it is possible to move from that to doing more journalism.

Listings

Almost every paper, from small local papers to nationals, now has extensive arts and entertainment listings sections. In some cases these are taken directly from a listings agency, which provides the same material to a number of subscribers. Most nationals produce big TV magazines at the weekend, with interviews and features about stars and new shows.

The broadsheets have comprehensive separate sections, the best known of which is probably *The Guardian*'s *The Guide*, which carries details of film, theatre, concerts, rock gigs, clubs and comedy venues, as well as TV listings. Working on the listings can be a good way to get into journalism, especially if you have a good eye for detail. There are several senior journalists on national newspapers who started their careers as listings subs.

Gardening/food/travel/property

'Whose turn was it for the facilities trip? Bob had had the Bulgarian State non-Ferrous Metals Trust jamboree the previous month, and he'd had the Cosmonair inaugural to Saarbrucken himself. It was old Eddy's turn.

"Eddy," he said, "would you like a little jaunt to Trucial Oman?" '

Michael Frayn, *Towards the End of the Morning*

These 'lifestyle' sections are lucrative areas, especially for some papers, with spin-off extra sections at the weekends. Each section will have an editor, one or two staff members, and possibly a large pool of freelance contributors. Gardening and food and wine writing is generally, but unfortunately not always, done by experts.

The travel pages will probably be edited, and to a certain extent written, by people who know the travel industry well, but much of the travel writing will be done by other staff members on the paper. Travel companies offer free holidays in exchange for a review, and these are generally shared out among those on the travel desk, or the travel editor's friends. In most papers travel pieces now carry a line at the bottom 'X travelled as a guest of Horrendous Holidays,' so readers, if they wish, can take the piece with a pinch of salt. Most students and recent graduates have nowadays done some exciting and feature-worthy travelling, and would dearly like to see their experiences in print. But the reality is that it is very hard to get travel pieces into papers unless you are known to the travel editor.

The travel and property sections, however, may be good areas to try to get some work experience or even a job as a researcher, as they often require short items – houses next to rivers for sale, for example, or possibilities for horseriding in Spain, and so on. National newspapers add new sections all the time: health perhaps, or a section about events and work in public and charity sectors. When these new sections start up they can be a very good place for work experience, as the new team might well need some people running around in an editorial assistant role until their work schemes get properly organised. If that goes well, then it could lead to a job. Special one-off sections might also provide an opportunity for a bit of freelance work: some broadsheets run gap-year travel sections in the summer, and might take a piece from a student.

Gossip columns/diaries

This is a huge growth area. Nearly every paper now has several gossip columns. Some are called diaries, but they are all basically a collection of small anecdotes about well-known people. The general public now has an insatiable interest in the minutiae of the lives of the rich and famous – witness the number of new and very successful magazines devoted to little else. In every national paper, apart from the *Financial Times*, a great deal of this material appears on the news pages: rock star buys new house, footballer wears hairband, film star's toddler has birthday party. So the gossip columns are left with the even more inconsequential stories: two soap stars go clubbing, one celeb says something rude about another. Thus it becomes even more important that they are written in a very sharp and clever way. So although a team of people may work on these columns, the diary editor will probably rewrite, or at least put his or her touch on each story, to give the whole thing a personal feel.

Junior jobs on these diaries, (the *Evening Standard*'s *Londoner's Diary* has a team of four) can be a good way into journalism. A recent graduate might be given the chance to go to book launches, celebrity lectures, fashion events and so on, and at first be paid for what she can get into the diary. Reporters on these diaries find themselves going to several parties every evening, in the hope that they will be around to witness, say, one celeb throwing a glass of wine over another.

The diary writer on a local paper which has a good selection of the rich and famous in its patch has a much easier time of it than one who does not. In the latter case, the poor diarist will be scratching round looking for stories among local councillors and village fetes.

Stand-alone sections: Sport and Business

Sport

> '"And none of your 'last analysis' or 'subsequent developments'," said the sports editor. 'This is for the *reading* public.'
>
> Patrick Campbell, Free for All,
> in the *P-P-Penguin Patrick Campbell*

Many people buy papers almost entirely for the sport. It is well documented that large numbers of readers, mostly men, turn first to the back pages of a paper to read the sports section and then work forwards. The deadlines of the complex regional editions of some tabloids depend almost entirely on the timings of football results.

All newspapers apart from the *Financial Times* now have very big sport sections, which, in the case of tabloids, fill up large sections of the back of the paper. Sometimes the sports section appears separately every day, or sometimes on Saturdays and Mondays, the biggest news days for football. The sports sections are almost complete newspapers in their own right, with an editor, deputy, news editors, columnists and their own subbing and production teams. The dailies are extremely busy towards the end of the week getting ready for the big Saturday edition, the Sundays are busy on Saturday actually getting as much coverage of the day into the next day's paper, and the dailies are busy again on Sundays doing the same for Monday. At these times they take on large numbers of casual reporters and subs. For a keen would-be sports journalist these can give good opportunities for work experience and shifts. Of course it is also the case that there are plenty of young people fascinated by sport who want these jobs. Accuracy and attention to detail are extremely important in sports subbing and reporting. A news reporter hopes to tell readers something they don't know, but this is often very far from the case with sports reporting. Many of the readers of match reports saw the same match, and are at least as knowledgeable about the team and its affairs as the reporter. They will spot errors, and not forgive them.

For many teenagers or students, the idea of going to a premiership match, sitting in one of the best seats (the press box), for which they have not paid, watching the match, then having the chance to sound off about it in print afterwards *and getting paid for it* sounds like heaven. Many sports journalists are extremely happy in their work, and never want to report anything but sport. But it can also be quite stressful: for example, reporters on morning papers attending an evening match often have to write most of the story on the way *to* the match, preparing two intros, one with each outcome. Then they slot in a few (accurate) points from the game, and phone or email the story almost before the match is over.

Business and personal finance

Again, on the broadsheets the business pages are almost a separate operation, with an editor, news editor, and dedicated production team. It is a growth area on broadsheet newspapers, so for first and second jobbers who have acquired some knowledge of business and finance, or can learn quickly, it can be a very good place to start in journalism. Many reporters become fascinated by the world of big business, although, as the former *Financial Times* editor Richard Lambert has acknowledged, genuine investigative work on the doings of big business has recently been lacking, for example in the Enron affair. The big regional papers also have business sections, with a dedicated team of reporters who will get to know about and then report on local businesses.

Possibly slightly less exciting than business is personal finance – reporting on mortgages, pension funds, options for savings accounts and investments. But again, for someone who knows about it, or is prepared to learn, the jobs are there.

Salaries on business sections are often slightly higher than for other reporting jobs. There may be many reasons for this: to compensate reporters for not being allowed to own shares, to bring their salaries more (but not very much more) into line with the salaries of their contacts in the City, or because there is simply a shortage of good business reporters.

Tabloids cover business and personal finance, but generally with a fraction of the space, and a fraction of the personnel that the broadsheets have. Business reporters on the redtops generally write stories about issues that will directly affect or interest their general readers. So they might write about the shares of household names, Manchester United, or Marks & Spencer, or they will explain how the euro will affect readers' holiday money.

The senior editorial team

'I did not come all this way not to interfere.'

Rupert Murdoch, in 1970, quoted by Stafford Somerfield,
then editor of the *News of the World*,
in his book *Banner Headlines*

'When you find yourself trapped in a cage with a tiger, you quickly learn in which direction to stroke its fur.'

Chinese proverb

Some years ago the *New Statesman* was looking for a new editor. It was a very democratic set-up and so the staff had some say in the matter and had difficulty agreeing who should be asked to take on the job. The story goes that at one point one staff member questioned whether they needed an editor at all, since the previous one had been something of a figurehead and was not too involved in the day-to-day work. The answer came 'Yes of course we do, because the editor is the one who goes to jail.'

It is true that the final responsibility for the entire publication resides with the editor, and yes, if a major lawsuit were lost, it might be the editor who would go to jail. This hasn't happened in recent history, but it seems clear that most editors have enough else to worry about. The British press is the most competitive in the world, and there is constant pressure to keep circulation up, beat the opposition, and in some cases at least, to satisfy a highly demanding proprietor. Only the editors themselves know how much pressure they are under from their bosses, but stories about press barons abound and Evelyn Waugh's Lord Copper in *Scoop* is a brilliant comic character partly because he is probably so near to real life. Rupert Murdoch mentioned the above Chinese proverb when paying tribute to Edward Pickering at his memorial service in December 2003. Pickering, a former editor of *The Daily Express*, had worked with Murdoch and had been his mentor for 50 years; he used to quote this proverb when asked about his relationships with proprietors. Murdoch modestly claimed that Pickering was referring only to their lordships Harmsworth and Beaverbrook, for whom he had also worked.

In a way, the debate about press barons' influence is a pointless one. Since they appoint the editor, it follows that they are going to appoint someone who is at least going to try to satisfy the boss. The only two nationals entirely free of a Lord Copper figure are *The Guardian* and *The Observer*, both owned by the independent Scott Trust. The well-known press barons are those whose companies own the nationals, but local papers are also regularly swallowed up by larger organisations. While those who run these companies may have no interest in having tea at 10 Downing Street, or seeking to influence editorial policy, they are still in charge of the balance sheet and thus affect the workings of the newsroom. Their main influence, rather than being over editorial policy, is probably over balance sheets. The big companies' drive for profits has certainly kept the wages of regional journalists quite low.

What do editors do?

On a small publication the editor would probably do the work of features editor and chief sub, news editing, designing pages, organising features and selecting pictures. Where there is a large staff, however, the editor's job is team leader, holding meetings with various groups (news, features, etc.) having ideas, encouraging people and generally getting the best people to do the various jobs.

Some national newspapers have or have had very flamboyant editors (Andrew Neil on *The Sunday Times*, Kelvin MacKenzie on *The Sun*) who seemed to see their role, among others, as raising the profile of the paper. Certainly Kelvin MacKenzie was a far cry from Michael Frayn's editor of his fictional paper in *Towards the End of the Morning*, who creeps silently into his office and communicates occasionally with his staff by letter. There were editors like that then: at one stage in the 1970s William Rees-Mogg decided to have a lunch with some of his fairly senior sub-editors at *The Times*. He had to be introduced to them all one by one, as most of them he had never met.

Nowadays most national editors spend at least part of the afternoon and early evening on the back bench, and are involved in many of the decisions about the coverage of major stories, the front page splash, headline and picture.

The deputy editor would also be involved and would stand in for the editor when he is on holiday or away. And many nationals have various associate editors, assistant editors and executive editors. Many of these will be senior political advisers, writing comment or leader columns. Others may be senior production journalists, and some may have been given these titles to lure them to the paper, because there was no other title available.

At least one national newspaper and some high-profile magazines have an editor-at-large, although it is not entirely clear what that involves. It is a title from the United States, where many big publications have editors-at-large, who seem to spend their time wining, dining and politicking. Not so long ago one national editor suddenly found himself with the title 'Editor Emeritus'. The apocryphal story is that he asked his press baron boss what this meant, and was told: 'E for exit, and meritus because you deserve it.'

Editors in Fleet Street, especially on the tabloids, come and go fairly quickly, but they seem to pop up again elsewhere quite often, and with any luck they will have arranged a contract with a comfortable financial parachute. No modern editor will ever match the record of the legendary C P Scott of the then *Manchester Guardian*, who became editor in 1872 and held the job for 57 years, still cycling home at 78 after a long night's work. It was Scott who wrote the famous aphorism: 'Comment is free, but facts are sacred', and gave his name to the Scott Trust which still owns *The Guardian*. But Scott owned the paper himself during the second half of his tenure, so he had no Lord Copper breathing down his neck.

Luke David, local paper reporter

Luke David, a reporter for the *Hampstead and Highgate Express*, gave up a successful career in an investment bank to follow his childhood dream and become a journalist. He always wanted to be a journalist because he wanted to have an insider view on everything that happened in the world.

Luke did a degree in International Relations at Westminster University and went on to do a Masters in International Politics at the School of Oriental and African Studies in London. He started working in an investment bank, an experience he describes as 'boring and dry'.

After two years, he decided to quit the job and look for an opportunity in journalism. It meant half the salary, but a more interesting job. A junior reporter on the *Ham and High* would earn about £16,000 in 2003. 'Money was not a driving factor as I have paid my student loans off and have bought a flat with my previous salary. Also £16,000 is the bottom of the food chain in journalism - the only way is up,' Luke says.

He took a five-month course at Harlow College, where he gained a pre-entry certificate, through the National Council for the Training of Journalists. The course taught him the basic things about journalism: shorthand, practical journalism, subbing, law and public affairs.

Luke already had some experience in journalism. While at university, he did a month's work experience at *The Independent*. Later, during his journalism course, he worked one day a week at the *Ham and High*. It was here that he found a job as a reporter. He knows he was very lucky to get this job immediately after he finished his diploma, and he never had to apply for any other one. Luke says that the first time he published an article he was really excited and he told all his friends about it.

Luke enjoys his work and is glad he dropped out of investment banking. Unlike some journalists, he feels that the work is not interfering with his personal life. 'At least, at this level, it isn't,' he says, 'because I'm working in a local newspaper'. He writes about anything that happens in the Hampstead area, from crime to plans for developments in the area to stories about famous people who live in Hampstead.

He says he occasionally finds the little local stories dull, but they attract some readers. The best part of the job, he says, is that journalists are allowed to be nosy. 'People expect you to be nosy,' he says 'and they don't mind if you actually are!'

He believes that it is obvious when a story has been done on the phone rather than face to face with an interviewee, so he likes to spend at least one day a week out of the office meeting people and digging up stories in his area.

After about two years on the paper he will take the NCTJ final National Certificate Examination. He must pass 100 words a minute at shorthand before he can enter, and prepare a logbook and portfolio with examples of a variety of reporting.

Luke usually works from 9:30 am to 6 pm. He says these hours are quite good compared to the average working hours in a national newspaper. Nevertheless, he would like to work on a national broadsheet in the future. 'That's what people who work in local press do. They work a couple of years in a local newspaper and then they move into the nationals,' he says. He already does Sunday freelance shifts for the *Daily Mirror*.

Luke would like to work either on *The Times* or *The Guardian* because he thinks their stories are more in-depth and he likes their style. In the future he would also like to write investigative material rather than just news stories. He says it is much more interesting to follow a story for some months than just write it up in an afternoon.

When asked about the most important quality for any would-be journalist, the answer comes straight away, in just one simple word: 'perseverance'.

Interview by Diogo Lemos

Niall Couper, national newspaper sports journalist

Nominated for Student Journalist of the Year in 1995 and now flying high at *The Independent*, Niall Couper is a journalist with the world at his feet.

Niall has worked hard to put himself in a good position by working for university newspapers, local publications, and starting on the bottom rung at *The Independent*. He completed a degree in Politics at Lancaster University, and a newspaper journalism postgraduate course at City University, London.

'I'd always wanted to get into journalism,' he said. 'After my degree, I did a teacher-training course and spent some time as a supply teacher. But I was doing shifts on local papers and on local radio stations. By then, I'd caught the buzz for news.' He said: 'I got a major buzz from news, and from editing. I worked on sports at the *Highbury and Islington Express*, and it was giving me such an unusual feeling that I knew I had to do it.'

He then followed the usual route of doing weekend shifts on national sports desks before landing his job at *The Independent*, where he now covers a variety of roles. 'I'm working six roles at the minute. Depending what they need me for, I could be night sports editor, sub-editing or any other number of jobs.'

But his flexibility and hard work have served him well. His position is directly below senior management, and this has made his life easier. 'It has taken me two years to get in to a good place at *The Independent*. At first, your social life goes out of the window and you have to work strange hours, but it's worth it in the end. I can work more of the shifts I want now.'

Sport is not where Niall wanted to make his name. 'I really wanted to be Roger Cook. I wanted to do investigative journalism. I ended up covering sport by accident, but I'm enjoying it.'

Working in sport has led him into the world of books and magazines, where he sees his future. He has published *The Spirit of Wimbledon*, a history of Wimbledon FC and the breakaway supporters' club, AFC Wimbledon, where he is editor of the match-day programme. When the financially troubled Wimbledon FC moved to Milton Keynes, angry fans in South London formed the breakaway AFC Wimbledon. Niall, a lifelong fan of the club, produced a book of interviews and commentary covering the original club's history from 1922 to a Cup Final win, to the sad day when it departed 70 miles north.

'Writing the book was a fun experience. I got to interview nearly 100 ex-players, managers and fans, and the book launch was an amazing experience. We had over 300 people turn up, and I didn't have enough time to sign all the books. I was signing four or five a minute and there was only just enough time to write my name.

'I'm more into the idea of moving towards books and magazines. You have far more freedom, and you get to make your own hours. Plus I prefer interviewing. Last year, I was doing stupid amounts of work with the book and the programme, but it's good fun and highly rewarding.'

However, the work for AFC Wimbledon has also led Niall into trouble. 'Charles Koppel [Wimbledon FC Chairman] has caused me a lot of grief. He's tried to sue me twice because of my work with AFC Wimbledon. 'But every time I've been in trouble, my editor's given me support, and for that I'm really grateful.'

Niall has only one regret – not pushing into news. But with ideas for books, and the possibility of moving up the ladder at *The Independent*, the future is bright.

Interview by David Pittman

3

Magazines

- *Consumer magazines*
- *B2B or trade magazines*
- *Contract publishing*
- *newsletters*
- *Other magazines*
- *The jobs*

'Once Snape had turned his back on them to write up the ingredients of today's potion on the blackboard, Hermione hastily riffled through the magazine under the desk. At last, in the centre pages, Hermione found what they were looking for. Harry and Ron leant in closer. A colour photograph of Harry headed a short piece entitled HARRY POTTER'S SECRET HEARTACHE:

a boy like no other, perhaps – yet a boy suffering all the usual pangs of adolescence, writes Rita Skeeter.....'

J K Rowling, *Harry Potter and the Goblet of Fire*

More than 9,000 magazines are published in the UK. They range from high-profile titles such as *Vogue, Glamour,* and *The Economist* (although it calls itself a newspaper), to such titles as *Meat Trades Journal, Plastics and Rubber Monthly* and *Fancy Fowl.* There aren't any magazines quite like Rita Skeeter's *Witch Weekly,* however, because although there are plenty about celebrities, they all tend to present their subjects in a positive light. The fictional *Witch Weekly* seems to be *Private Eye* with added cake recipes – an unlikely combination.

The magazine industry is expanding all the time, with new titles being launched regularly, covering every specialised area one could think of, and plenty one would never have thought of. In terms of first jobs, magazines in general pay rather better than local papers. But many of them operate with a very small staff who will not have the time or the inclination to train someone. On many magazines almost all the big features are done by freelances, experienced journalists who have developed knowledge and skills in particular areas. Rita Skeeter is probably one such, since she writes for the *Daily Prophet* as well.

On a small specialist magazine a staff journalist might not write major features. He or she will be expected to chase up news items one day, write a short feature another, and design a page another day. Occasionally, staff journalists may be called upon to design adverts, something the National Union of Journalists would not have been happy about a few years ago, but which is probably quite common on some small magazines. So first jobbers on such magazines have to be multi-skilled. You are far more likely to get work if you have followed a training course, are a reasonably competent news reporter, and can use desktop publishing software such as QuarkXPress. In fact, the huge growth in small magazines may be partly due to the large pool of young people coming off journalism courses who have reasonable knowledge of the above areas and can start contributing usefully to the magazine from day one.

There are three main categories of magazine.

Consumer magazines

These are the highest-profile magazines, the ones you buy in a newsagent. They are defined generally as those magazines which provide leisure-time information and entertainment. That is, they are about consuming things, from make-up to holidays to sun-dried tomatoes. There are more than 3,000 of them, with new ones being launched all the time, although a few fall by the wayside every year. They often contain a large amount of lucrative advertising, whether for Armani (*Vogue*) or grand conservatories (*Gardens Illustrated*). This group includes special-interest magazines (see below) but some of these are a very different type of publication from the high-profile ones.

There must be a hundred or so well-known consumer magazines, everything from *Cosmopolitan* to *Woman, Take a Break* and *FHM*. Some of these are also known as **glossies** because of the quality paper on which they are printed, which makes the photos and the advertising look very smart. Until the late 1980s the majority of the best-known ones, apart from the music magazines, were targeted at women. But in the past 15 years or so there has been an explosion in magazines aimed at men, from *Loaded* to *Maxim* to *Jack*. The men's market has been a roller-coaster, with some magazines experiencing sudden great successes and just as suddenly crashing down the circulation charts. Men are apparently very fickle, and buy whichever one they like the look of each month, rather than becoming loyal to one particular magazine. The magazines seem to have had some difficulty in establishing themselves as 'badge products' – the marketing jargon for a publication that readers buy not just because they want to read what it offers, but because reading the magazine says something about them. Apparently women are more likely to buy a magazine partly because it is a badge product.

All these magazines offer huge (in many cases half-price) discounts to those who subscribe for a year and receive them through the post. Sending *Vogue* through the post is not cheap, but distributing it in the conventional way isn't cheap either, and the publisher has the great advantage of locking the reader in for a year. The possibility that there may soon be postage pricing bands based on size may have a serious effect on the distribution costs of these magazines.

Many glossies have expensively photographed and lavishly produced advertising. The highest-profile magazines often do not have such large circulations as many other publications, but they get a big proportion of their revenue from advertising. The front half of *Country Life*, for example, is filled with adverts for property and antiques. The niche market is very important as well; advertisers in *Vogue* know they will reach not only a high proportion of big spenders on fashion, but also everyone who matters in the fashion trade.

A slightly different section of the consumer market is the group of **specialist** or **special interest magazines**. These are aimed at people with a particular interest in one area, whether it is cars, computers, photography, gardening or antiques. There is a magazine for everything, from *Classic Stitches* to *Toy Soldiers and Toy Figures* to *Opera Now*. Again, these titles are about consuming, whether it is buying a horse or an opera ticket. Many of them appear on the newsstands, but some are available only on subscription. Some have a very small staff, perhaps only an editor, a deputy whose main role might be commissioning features from freelances and specialists, and one other reporter. The editor and the deputy might do all the design as well.

These are good areas for jobs, but in some cases specialist knowledge is needed. For example, because of the huge scope for error with the names of plants, or characters in baroque opera, you are unlikely to get a job on a gardening or music magazine without some special knowledge. *The Garden*, the Royal Horticultural Society's magazine, has a scheme where it regularly takes on a trainee journalist, but it is always someone with a horticultural qualification rather than a journalistic one.

Other less specialised publications may well take first or second jobbers who have proved they can report accurately, and more particularly, sub and design pages. Some of the areas these magazines cover are so esoteric that the editor is unlikely to find a would-be journalist who knows, say, about wristwatches or wood-carving. In such a case, he might well rather have someone who can sub and design well using QuarkXPress, and rely on the contributors to get the facts about the hobby right. It is not too difficult to move around this area, although if you have got a job on, say, a gardening magazine because of your knowledge in that area you will need to think carefully about your transferable skills, and work them up, if you want to move into another area of magazines.

B2B or trade magazines

This means 'business to business', and is what used to be called trade magazines. They are magazines about a particular sector or industry or service provision, for the people who work in that sector. *Press Gazette* is for journalists about journalism, *Rail News* is about the rail industry for those who work in it, and so on.

There are around 5,700 of these magazines. The number has gone up by 26 per cent since 1990, and it seems likely to rise still further. They often have a great deal of lucrative recruitment advertising, and in many cases, have become almost the only place to advertise. There is a threat to one group of these magazines however, because the NHS may set up a website to publicise jobs within the NHS, which could affect the advertising revenue of the many titles aimed at doctors, nurses and health workers. Many of these magazines make excellent places for first jobs or work experience as they often carry a lot of small news items about what is going on in their area, and producing them is the kind of work a first jobber or work experience person can do. The titles range from *Petroleum Economist* to *Laundry and Dry Cleaning News*. But don't worry that you might end up reporting about industrial washing machines for the rest of your life. The great thing about B2B magazines, for someone just starting in journalism, is that the skills are transferable. Reporters, subs and designers move around from magazine to magazine, and once they have proved they can report accurately on the doings of one industry, they move to report a completely different one. The same applies to the subs and designers. One former student who started on *Meat Trades Journal* has now moved to *Pulse*, a highly respected magazine for doctors.

One career progression in B2B magazines then, might involve moving around different areas, and eventually becoming editor on one magazine then, with those editing skills, moving to becoming editor of a bigger magazine. Many of these magazines are published by one of the handful of big publishing companies, including EMAP, Haymarket, Reed and Quantum. There are good career progressions available within these companies, with journalists often moving from one title to another quite different one. Another career progression might be, having gained a good knowledge of a sector, moving into public relations for a firm in that sector. Having learned about an industry, one could also progress by moving to a big regional or national paper as a specialist. This is particularly the case with those working on medical magazines, and also with transport or agriculture. Reporters on specialist B2B magazines covering some industries – say mining or electronics – are particularly well placed to try for jobs on the *Financial Times*, where they have specialists covering every industry.

Many of the B2B magazines provide excellent work experience opportunities. If you are interested in fashion or beauty, for example, it might be far better to try to do some work experience at *Drapers* or *Hairdressers' Journal* before trying *Vogue*. Many of the publishing houses involved in B2B have other spin-off activities, such as organising conferences, publishing business directories and producing new media products such as reference CDs. So another possible career path would be to move into a semi-managerial role in these areas.

B2B magazines vary in the way they operate: some have a controlled circulation (i.e. a magazine may go to all GPs, but to no one else) or they can be requested circulation – for example, you are an accountant and you ask to get a particular magazine. This gives the publishers another spin-off activity – they might sell on the lists of accountants who have asked for the magazine. Some of the biggest B2B magazines are simply sold over the counter to consumers, among them *Press Gazette* and *The Times Educational Supplement.*

Nerys Hairon, reporter, *Pulse Magazine*

Nerys Hairon, the Senior General News Reporter at *Pulse Magazine* at 29 years old, is truly one of City University's many success stories, recently winning a Special Commendation in the Trade News category of the Norwich Union Healthcare Medical Journalism Awards 2003.

She studied at Oxford University for her main degree in Modern Languages, and then found her way on to a course at City. After completing a postgraduate diploma in Newspaper Journalism, her first job was at *The Wharf,* the newspaper that covers Canary Wharf in London.

'My first job was at *The Wharf* for just over six months. I got it because I knew someone else from City who said they were still looking for people.' Nerys suffered some bullying there because she is partially sighted. She said there was a feeling that she should be grateful for the job because she couldn't see properly.

This seems to have been the only major problem she has faced in the world of journalism, and she hopes it will stay that way. She said of her disability: 'It's just awkward in job interviews because I feel I have to tell people about it, and then I am worried they may be hesitant to employ me.' She believes that, with age and experience, this should cease to be a problem. From *The Wharf*, Nerys went to the *Meat Trades Journal*.

She applied unsuccessfully to the *Press Gazette*, but found a position at the *Meat Trades Journal*, which is run by the same company. Nerys found that the subject area was interesting, and the office was friendly and informal. 'I also had the opportunity to travel around Europe and write a wide range of stuff including news, features, news features, comments, focus pieces, investigations and eight-page specials.' She was promoted to News Editor and learned to commission, budget and manage staff. From the *Meat Trades Journal*, Nerys went to *Pulse*, and has never looked back.

Moving between totally different B2B publications does not seem to have been a problem. Indeed she said: 'It is fairly easy. I didn't know anything about health when I started at *Pulse*, but have just learnt it. When you have done one specialist area, I think it shows that you can learn quickly.'

Nerys has striven towards a career in journalism all of her life; this much is obvious from the amount of effort and interest she has put into achieving it. The reasons she chose to study journalism are varied: 'I did a lot of work experience at my local paper before City [University,] and did loads of journalism there when I was a teenager. I worked for the local youth supplement in Jersey where I grew up. I have always been interested in writing, current affairs, social issues and politics.' But the one thing that stands out, and really gives a clue to the woman behind the journalist, is her final reason for choosing journalism: 'I also really like the day to day aspects of the job. And being nosey!'

Pulse is very widely read among GPs and has a controlled circulation of around 40,000. 'I enjoy my job loads, it's very good experience and interesting too if you interested in health policy,' she says. A normal working day begins at around 9.15 am and finishes at around 5.15 pm, although she admits that she is usually in the office till much later: 'I tend to have to work till 5.30pm or 6pm, or even later. I have been at BMA House till 11pm on contract night, but we get lieu time for that.'

As Senior General News Reporter, Nerys's day-to-day duties vary. Most days, she is expected to find her own stories on GP political issues, call doctors to do phone interviews, check websites for news stories, and go to press conferences at BMA House and the Department of Health. She admits that some of her tasks are a bit routine, and there are pressures involved in satisfying different senior people. Sometimes she finds herself looking for picture stories when there aren't any to be found, or being cross-examined over a really complicated story. 'Reading really boring reports and not getting stories in or having them cut when you've spent ages on them are other things, but the hardest and probably worst thing of all is having to find stories when there simply aren't any!'

Having just received awards for her work and a salary bonus, Nerys was earning £28,000 a year at the age of 29, so she feels she cannot complain. 'There are some amazing things about working here – getting to go to conferences, staying in swanky hotels, taking contacts out for dinner to the OXO Tower, and getting the chance to give BMA people and health ministers a good grilling – these are the best parts of my job. I also enjoy going to briefings and getting on really well with regular contacts and getting good stories out of them.' Then she adds, 'Oh yes – and writing stories and getting awards for them – two this year.'

And where does she see herself in five years? 'I'm not entirely sure. I hope I'll be working for a national in either news or features, or a consumer magazine or even possibly freelancing on a wide range of stuff.' Perhaps working as a health correspondent on a national? 'Yes, in an ideal world, but it's just getting the opportunity.' It is clear that to Nerys journalism, above all else, is the thing she enjoys the most about her job.

Interview by Sarah Ardley

Helen McCormick: B2B features editor

Working on a small highly specialised B2B magazine has enabled Helen McCormick to rise through the ranks to become features editor within two years of starting in journalism.

Helen had always enjoyed writing and after her degree she took the Postgraduate Newspaper Diploma at City University. When the course ended she trawled through *The Guardian*'s media supplement and applied for nearly every job under the sun before landing her first job as a reporter on the newly-launched weekly *Mortgage Strategy* in September 2001. In June 2003 she was made the Features Editor of the publication, which has expanded rapidly from 28 pages when it was launched to 56 pages two years later. The staff, too, grew in that time from three to seven.

Helen is the first to admit that *Mortgage Strategy* may not sound the most riveting title, but the mortgage market is booming at the moment and that means there is plenty to write about. The magazine is aimed at professionals in the mortgage industry, and has a controlled circulation of about 11,000. It is free to anyone who spends at least 20% of their time on mortgage broking. For any other interested parties it is available at a price of £3.95. It is fully funded by advertising.

The job allows Helen to write both news and feature articles. She works fairly normal office hours, finishing at 5.30 with a Friday deadline. Helen's workload includes on average one main feature of 4,000 words a month, and a weekly company profile. She also commissions features and edits the other 12 feature pages. There are a couple of more light-hearted pages, including a CV page and a diary column that Helen does. Most of the contributors are professionals in the industry, rather than writers, and their copy can be quite entertaining. Helen enjoys the editing process, although she didn't expect to. The art editor designs the pages, but all the staff are involved in coming up with ideas for the front page.

There are perks to the job: in the run-up to Christmas she spent a day being pampered at The Sanctuary spa in London, and she goes to a lot of lunches and has a fair number of days out, including big sports fixtures and parties.

Helen has been exploring freelance work, selling an exclusive to the *Daily Mail*, and she has recently finished her first piece for *The Daily Telegraph*. Her piece for the *Mail* was about how much debt young people are getting into: 'It is very rare for such a consumer-friendly story to come up,' she said.

Because the mortgage world is relatively small, Helen's little black contacts book is almost full and it is an invaluable tool in the job. It is still the case that it's not what you know but who you know.

In five years' time Helen hopes to have left the mortgage world behind her and entered the more cut-throat world of the nationals. Although *Mortgage Strategy* has allowed her to develop in a small environment she feels it may be time to venture into the wider world. But she says she would move only to somewhere really promising, as she feels she is progressing well where she is. Be it newspapers or magazines Helen wishes to stay on the weeklies rather than the monthlies because they are faster and have shorter deadlines, something Helen has grown to love.

The majority of the people she works with took similar routes to Helen. They nearly all have either an undergraduate or postgraduate qualification in journalism. But she added that however much college lecturers can teach you, six months in the industry can show you a great deal more.

Interview by Jo Knight

Contract publishing

A contract magazine is one published on behalf of a third party (such as a business, a pressure group, a charity, or society), to be given or sold to their customers or supporters. Britain's largest circulation magazine, *Sky Customer Magazine*, for those with (fairly new) satellite dishes, falls into this category. In fact the top five magazines in terms of circulation are all in this category. Again, these magazines are about consuming things – TV programmes or canapés – so some regard them as falling into the broad category of consumer magazines. And while all contract magazines are customer magazines, not all customer magazines are published on a contract. In some cases the society or pressure group publishes its own.

Customer publishing is a relatively new market. It started only about 30 years ago with in-flight magazines, and the early ones were not great in terms of writing and design, nor were they well regarded in the world of journalism. Now there are hundreds of different titles, many extremely well produced, with plenty of good writing. Many are now highly respected, not least because of their success. Journalists move around a great deal from these magazines to general lifestyle or specialist publications. The big firms which publish several of them also tend to move staff around as well. Someone who has been seen to edit one magazine successfully might be asked to take on another less successful title in a completely different area.

Obviously these companies are very commercial and they are keen to sell their particular brand to the reader. So, for example, the Waitrose magazine is all about confirming to its readers that they are right to shop at Waitrose. Some storecards have software enabling them to track what the holder buys, and this information can then be related back to see if coverage in the associated magazine persuaded the customer to make a particular purchase. As the publications come from the business or organisation's promotional budget, it wants to see value for money. *Heritage* magazine, sent to members of English Heritage, for instance, needs to show that more people visited a particular heritage site specifically because of the magazine.

Many of these magazines are about a particular hobby or enthusiasm – John Brown Citrus, for example, publishes several magazines aimed at owners of Ford cars. So they would make a very good first work experience slot for someone with a particular interest in cars.

It is hard to get good work experience on a top newsstand fashion and beauty magazine, but *Spirit* (for Superdrug card holders) or *Health and Beauty* (Boots) might be a good start. Some of these publications also have good websites, which might be another area for work experience.

Some publishing houses also produce magazines for charities, societies, or other pressure groups to distribute to members. Some of the very big charities publish their own – the Royal Horticultural Society publishes *The Garden* and The National Trust publishes its own magazine, for example.

Contracts for publishing these customer magazines seem to come and go fairly rapidly. One minute a big organisation publishes its own magazine, the next thing a contract firm is doing it, and then just as suddenly it is taken back in-house. This can add to the general insecurity for people working on them.

BBC Magazines, the BBC's big empire, is a mixture of customer and consumer publishing. Its magazines are available on newsstands, but at the same time they are linked to and promote some of the BBC's programmes, and in some cases the magazines are a spin-off from the programmes.

newsletters

A newsletter is generally defined as a publication that goes to its readers only on subscription, and which is financed entirely by that subscription; that is, it has no advertising. Newsletters are at one end of the B2B market, and are generally about some aspect of the world of finance. For example, they distribute prices of commodities, business intelligence about the market, and political and other news which might affect the market. The difference between them and, say, the *Press Gazette* is that the latter might be useful in work terms, but is mainly of interest to its readers. A newsletter is probably going to be an essential tool enabling its readers to do their jobs. They are generally very expensive, and are paid for by companies, rather than individuals.

There was a big increase in the number of newsletters when desktop publishing became widespread about 30 or so years ago. For someone with a great deal of knowledge about a certain market, such as oil, and a great many contacts in that market, they were obviously cheap to set up. The staff can be small because no advertising team is needed, and the people who have paid a substantial subscription just want the facts – they don't need fancy design or pictures. Now the market is being rationalised and many of the small ones are selling out to bigger firms, probably making considerable sums of money for the people who started them up. But generally they keep their own identities, which have become known and are trusted by the subscribers. Most of these newsletters are now distributed by email or via the web, but they are included in this chapter because they do not fit into the category of online journalism like the BBC or *Guardian* sites. The electronic distribution is simply a way of issuing the information.

Electronic distribution has made life easier for the publishers, indeed some now charge more if the subscriber insists on a paper copy of the newsletter. But there have been headaches too: it is very easy for a single subscriber to forward the whole thing to everyone else in a big organisation. Publishers are keeping a close eye on this, and there have been threats of court action unless the recipient pays a licence fee to distribute the material.

The best-known publications are those from Standard and Poor's, and Moodys, which provide information on global financial markets; *Metal Bulletin*, which deals with commodities, and Platts and Argus, which both provide energy news. The Economist Intelligence Unit is a very big enterprise, providing masses of information to its subscribers about different countries, industries and markets. These newsletters are not well known outside their own areas, but they might well be worth investigating for a first or second job.

They employ teams of people who contact market participants all day, getting prices that are reported in the newsletter. They carry more traditional news, say about what OPEC is doing, or about politics in the Middle East. Work on a newsletter would be an excellent opportunity to acquire a great deal of knowledge about finance and politics. The pay is good, comparable with national newspapers and international agencies. The emphasis is obviously on accuracy and speed. You would need to be interested in, though not necessarily knowledgeable about, financial markets, and languages might be an advantage.

It is common to move from newsletters to the *FT*, Reuters and Bloomberg, and in the other direction. Almost all the work is reporting, as there is no real design or display involved. In that sense, because of the electronic distribution, the work is similar to that of a financial reporter at a news agency.

These jobs are sometimes advertised: the first thing to do would be to search around on their websites. They are also sometimes advertised in *The Guardian*. Journalists also get into this kind of work by word of mouth, or through work experience.

Other magazines

There are several thriving and high-profile political magazines; the best known are *The Economist*, the *New Statesman* and *The Spectator*. These are not very good places for first jobs, as the latter two are mostly made up of contributions from freelances, and there are no little bits of news or small feature subjects to be covered. *The Economist* and *Time* have large staffs, but these are generally all highly experienced journalists and the publications are not a very likely area for a first or second job. I generally warn against trying for work experience on these magazines, although I have known students, usually those who are very interested in politics, to have a good time.

Then there is the **ethnic press**, with titles such as *The Voice*, *New Nation*, *Asian Eye*, and other magazines for particular groups, such as *Gay Times* and the *Pink Paper*. There are at present nine publications aimed at the gay community. Some of them fall into the category known as **the alternative press** although this expression has perhaps not been very clearly defined. Some magazines which might have been alternative 20 years ago, such as *Private Eye*, seem fairly mainstream now. There are more of these than most people would think, and although some come and go fairly rapidly, they might make an excellent place for work experience or a first job. *The Guardian Media Directory* has a good list of them.

Another group of publications are the **in-house journals**, magazines run by large companies for their own employees. Sometimes they are actually produced in-house, but in many cases the magazine is produced by a contract publishing firm (see above) who can provide a better product. This is because they have a team of journalists working on several projects and they can make economies of scale and expertise.

There is a growing number of magazines aimed at, and usually written by, members of particular communities. Under this heading fall the many pop music and football fanzines, some printed, and some web-based. As desktop publishing becomes more sophisticated these 'zines' which 20 years ago would have looked very amateurish, now often look very smart. It is worth trying to get some writing into these if you have enough knowledge and interest in their particular area. But they are generally shoestring operations and would be a place to look for work experience and to get some cuttings, rather than a job.

There are **county magazines** outside London – *Dorset Life* etc., matched by their urban counterparts, the **glossy freebie magazines**, such as *The Angel* in Islington, and *The London Magazine*. All of these are basically vehicles for property advertising, but they do have some editorial.

Many **local councils** also run magazines, generally covering all their recent achievements. Ken Livingstone's eight-strong PR team at City Hall in London produces a very good newspaper with lots of information and positive PR about the mayor's activities.

Any of the above might make a good place to start in journalism or work experience. It is a matter of researching what there is, and realising that there is more journalism going on out there than can be seen on the average newsstand.

The jobs

This section is devoted mainly to the kind of work on magazines that relates to the words. There is more discussion about design, pictures, picture researching and graphics in Chapter 7.

There are different titles on various magazines for similar jobs. An assistant to the features editor might be doing what is basically a journalistic job when it sounds as though it is administrative. A commissioning editor might be someone quite senior and grand, or it might equally be a college leaver. A contributing editor doesn't usually edit anything. What follows is an outline of roughly what the jobs are, but bear in mind that on any particular magazine there may be slightly different titles for the same job, and people with the same title might be doing slightly different things.

To try to show what sort of jobs there are in magazines, I have taken two very different types of magazine which could be said to be at opposite ends of a spectrum. At one end is a B2B magazine which covers a particular industry, where there is quite a bit going on in terms of news, but also many opportunities for features about people and issues. At the other end is a big consumer glossy, which is full of features which are essentially about what to spend one's money on. Most magazines will fall somewhere on a spectrum between these two types.

The B2B magazine

The jobs on this kind of publication will be broadly similar to those on a newspaper. A big magazine will have a team of **reporters**, led by a **news editor**. B2B magazines often have sizeable reporting teams and this can be an excellent place for a first or second job. On a magazine covering a big, highly competitive world, *Estates Gazette*, for example, or *The Lawyer*, there will be a great deal of work for news reporters, talking to contacts, attending events and keeping abreast of developments in the industry. Some of the work will be following up press releases, but there should be plenty of opportunity to get good stories that are not PR-based.

On a smaller magazine one of the main roles of the most junior member of staff is often to fill a page or more with news items, culled from press releases and contacts. A reporter who gets to know the industry, and can bring in exclusive stories, will be highly valued. There are well-established career paths within these magazine firms, and reporters can work their way up to editor and then publisher. It is also possible to move to big regional or national papers, possibly as a specialist in the same field. But as we have said, good reporters can move to a completely different area of magazines as well.

Further across the spectrum towards the leisure magazine, reporting on specialised magazines is likely to be more diary or press release-based. There are probably not that many major scandals in the world of budgerigars, although if there were one, the editor would expect the reporter on *Cage and Aviary Birds* to discover it. On the whole, reporting on specialist magazines is likely to cover new products, 'how to' information about growing onions or treating yacht timber, competitions, meetings and shows.

There may be a small **features team** on the magazine, led by a **features editor**. Many of the reporters will also write features, reporting in depth on issues they may have uncovered in their news reporting. They may also write profiles, interviews with big players in the field, and even maybe comment columns. The features editor will also have a bank of freelances who either offer material for the features pages, or are commissioned to cover particular issues. There may well also be a couple of columns from people who are not full-time journalists but who work in the sector the magazine covers.

The magazine will have a design team, perhaps led by a **production editor** or an **art editor**. There are unlikely to be staff photographers, but there might be an assistant art or design person who commissions freelance photographers and graphic artists, and researches pictures.

The consumer glossy

Glossy magazines do not have reporters, in the sense of someone who sets out to find out some news. The emphasis for these magazines is on things to buy, things to do and places to go. *Vogue*, for example, does not cover developments in the fashion industry in the way that *Drapers* does. The editorial material in the big consumer magazines is about new fashions, new make-up, new spas and new restaurants, written up in the style of features. Whereas on a newspaper the jobs will be grouped in news and features, the jobs on magazines will be grouped in different ways, depending on what kind of magazine it is. A fashion magazine, for instance, will have separate teams covering fashion, beauty, and so on.

The team will consist of, say, the fashion editor, and possibly, senior to her, the fashion director. These people will not write very much, if anything, but will be expert at researching what is going to be the next big idea, spotting trends, and working out what kind of clothes to feature in the next issue. The fashion team will be responsible for getting material written, and more important, commissioning photographs.

Editorial material will often be written by freelances, who report to a **commissioning editor**. This is the person to whom freelances pitch ideas, or who contacts freelances asking them to write up ideas that have been put forward in editorial meetings. Plenty of freelances, even when they are extremely well established, have jaundiced views of commissioning editors, and in some cases the feeling is mutual. But somehow the two sides rub along enough to get the words into the magazine.

The title of contributing editor is rather puzzling. This person does not edit anything, and is probably not on the staff at all. It is a title given to a freelance, possibly on a contract, and possibly someone who is very well known, who writes a feature or two for every edition.

There is lots of work to be done by **editorial assistants**. They may have slightly different titles, and may be assigned to work with a particular team, depending on the size of the magazine. They are responsible for research, chasing up people and products, and making sure the facts about merchandise that appear in the magazine are correct. Many of the big glossies have a 'permanent' team of work experience people logging clothes as they come in and seeing that they are returned.

Wherever a magazine is on the spectrum, there will of course be an **editor**. Depending on the size of the magazine she may be very much a working editor, laying out pages, writing a column, perhaps even writing features. On a large magazine, however, as on a big newspaper, the editor's role will mainly be one of having creative ideas, and getting the best out of the team. Editors move around fairly quickly, and these moves are often reported in the *Press Gazette*. The emphasis, when a glossy appoints a new editor, is usually very much on whether the new editor is going to come in with lots of ideas.

In the magazine world there is a specialised role of **publisher**, which is not used all that much in the newspaper world. (One exception to this was Robert Maxwell, who, when he owned the Mirror Group, decreed that he should be addressed as Publisher: 'Yes Publisher, no Publisher', rather like 'Yes Prime Minister' or 'Thank you your Holiness'.) In a small set-up the publisher may also be the proprietor, the person who had the idea, and either put up the money or got someone to lend it. In bigger organisations the publisher is the one with the purse-strings who is responsible for strategic planning. It is possible to become publisher through the editorial side, and it is also possible to get there through the advertising and managerial side. Either way, the publisher is the equivalent of managing director in many other businesses.

Dan Rookwood: commissioning editor

The last few days of 2003 were pretty exciting for Dan Rookwood. After-show parties with The Strokes and Justin Timberlake during the weekend and dinner with the victorious England Rugby team on Monday night. Oh, and a day or two after that he started work at one of Britain's biggest men's lifestyles magazines, *Men's Health*, as commissioning editor.

His job combines writing and editing, as well as publicising the magazine and recruiting staff for it. The world of journalism has been treating him very kindly indeed. 'Being a journalist is a very attractive job with all the parties and the free stuff. It's a career where you get to do things that people in normal jobs only dream about.'

The attraction of journalism for this Liverpool-born lad began when he was 14. Unable to follow his dream of playing professional football, he embarked on the path of writing about it. This path would take him around the world and back again, to an Independent/NUS Student Sports Journalist of the Year award and what sounds like a very lively and satisfying career.

At Cambridge University, while studying Geography, he did a lot of student journalism. 'I spent far too much time playing sport and writing about sport, rather than concentrating on my degree.' It was at Cambridge that a somewhat cheeky letter to his journalistic idol, *The Daily Telegraph*'s sports columnist Henry Winter, brought him into the world of professional sports writing. Winter took him under his wing and showed him the ropes. It was an experience he would never forget.

Despite working on various student magazines while at university, he didn't have much experience working for professional titles. After leaving Cambridge, he knew this had to change. 'I wrote to every newspaper and magazine on the shelves at WH Smith. I then spent a whole summer doing work experience.'

This resulted in an impressive list of newspaper and magazine placements, including *GQ*, *The Daily* and *Sunday Telegraph*, *Four Four Two* magazine, *The Times* and the *Kent Messenger*. Then when travelling around Australasia, he managed to squeeze in time at the *Sunday Times* in Sydney, *The Australian* and the *Wellington Evening News*. It was the placement at *GQ*, however, which for him has brought the most reward. '*GQ* gave me a couple of really good contacts. One of them remembered me later and I worked freelance for him at *Maxim*, where I was Health and Beauty and Bar Editor. Then when he went to *Men's Health*, I went with him again.'

After cutting his teeth in placements, Dan arrived at City

University to do the Post-Graduate Diploma in Newspaper Journalism, but he soon found that life inside the classroom wasn't for him. 'I didn't really enjoy it. I felt that I didn't need to sit and hear about something I didn't need anyway. I thought a football journalist doesn't need to learn about local government.'

It was chance and another bold play, however, which brought him into the real world. While on work experience at *The Guardian*, he discovered there was a job going. He cheekily asked if he could apply, even though the deadline for applications was the week before. He was told that if he handed in a CV by the end of the day he would be considered, and ultimately, he got the job. So he finished his diploma while writing sports for *The Guardian*, supplementing his income with regular freelance work.

'This was my introduction to just how lucrative the freelance world can be [and] with a couple of notable exceptions, *The Guardian* understood and 'decriminalised' my clandestine freelance kerb-crawling.'

By now he had really found his calling: 'When I was published in *Four Four Two*, I was so happy because it was the magazine I read as a kid.'

The future for Dan isn't clear-cut, with both newspapers and magazines attractive and available options. 'I see myself as the Deputy Editor of a men's lifestyle magazine, like *Esquire*, or working on Premiership coverage for a Sunday national. My ideal job would be like A.A. Gill. He has the freedom to write what he wants, where he wants.'

'As long as the free stuff keeps coming, it doesn't really matter.'

Interview by David French

David Whitehouse: magazine staff writer

David Whitehouse leaped from writing pornography disguised as a woman for a text messaging company, to working as the only staff writer for *Jack* – the monthly men's magazine.

By the time he was 22, David had been working in the office for a year, with his own desk and own title, so there was no need to fight with freelances on what to write. *Jack* has a dozen or so full-time staff, excluding freelancers. *Jack* is very much at the high end of the men's market. 'I love my job, because it involves interviewing bands and actors,' said David, who also edits a number of sections in the magazine. He writes features on anything from films, to sport, to war crimes. The rhythm of a monthly magazine means you have to be thinking two months ahead all the time: in January you are writing features which your readers will see two months later.

David loves the job because of his lifelong interest in music, and because he felt that by working for magazines, there was the chance to travel with his passion and to meet famous people. He also writes previews of new TV series and programmes after interviewing the actors in them.

David, from Nuneaton, graduated from the London College of Printing with a BA Journalism degree at 21. 'Studying journalism for the first two years wasn't easy, as we had to study philosophy and history,' David said, adding that in the final year the students had to produce a newspaper every week, which was hard work. But he enjoyed it in the end. During his second year at college, he entered a student competition and wrote a piece that won him a month's work placement at the *Observer* magazine. After being given the choice between news and features, he chose to work at the features desk, writing about men's health.

His next job was at the *Evening Standard*, after he'd won another award for a piece on three major disasters of his life. With help from Melanie McFadyean, his course teacher at LCP, he managed to integrate three stories: on a heart attack he had suffered, on his house getting burned down, and on how he had chicken pox. He says he came up with a brilliant piece, and although unfortunately it never got published, he won a prize of £1,000 cash, which went on a holiday to Barcelona with a friend.

His first paid writing job, which he had seen advertised, was writing pornographic text messages. He masqueraded as a woman, replying to messages from lonely men. 'It was all a big lie,' he said. The job description called for someone who was 'creative, quick to think, and not offensive'. Users of the service paid £1 to receive a message, and another £1 to send a reply.

David worked part-time at this strange writing job for three years, during his time at college and for six months after graduation. 'I've applied for many jobs and I've learned that, as a journalist, you must face the facts that some jobs are not what you expect to get,' said David, whose main reason for taking the job was because he needed the money.

With text messaging far behind him, his future in magazines looks rosy. 'Ideally, I can see myself still working for magazines in the next five years, preferably on this one as the features editor, or I would like to edit my own magazine. My faraway dream is to write a book,' he said.

David advises journalism students to enter for as many awards as they can: 'Every journalist can write, but winning an award shows that you are a step ahead, and it makes you stand out.' He believes that if he hadn't won the awards he would never have gone this far in his career at such a young age. 'I was extremely lucky to win that award, and I don't think I could do any better if I had taken another route. If you don't stand out, I doubt any magazine company would take you.'

Interview by Nicole Tsang

Emma Morris: lifestyle magazine feature writer

Emma Morris from Edinburgh is a features writer for *Kitchens, Bedrooms and Bathrooms Magazine*, and she is also doing freelance work for a fact book called *Where to Ski and Snowboard*.

Emma first found out that she wanted to go into journalism around the age of 16 when she was in her second to last year of school. The students were asked to find an area to do work experience in, and she gave the *Edinburgh Evening News* a go. 'I had a great time there, and from then on I wanted to go into journalism,' she says.

At university, she did not do a journalism course. She decided to take the language route, and did English and French at Aberdeen University. Despite the choice not to do a straight journalism course, she did keep her interest for the profession alive and kicking. She wrote avidly for the student newspaper, and also got a feeling of the world of broadcasting when she did some work experience for Northsound Radio.

After her degree, Emma made a firm decision that journalism was what she wanted to get into. She jumped on a train to London, and headed straight for City University. Although she was clear that she wanted to work as a journalist, she had not decided on what type of journalism she wanted to pursue. So she went for the postgraduate newspaper journalism course at City University.

During her time at City University, she came to realise that writing for newspapers was not going to make her happy. Features were really what she was the most interested in. 'I enjoyed features more than news, because I could get deeper into the subjects. News was too strict,' she says. She did, however, decide to finish the newspaper journalism course and then follow the features path afterwards.

When Emma came to apply for her first paid job, she had quite an impressive CV to send off with her application. She had done work experience for *The Times*, the *Observer*, the *Scotsman*, *Edinburgh Evening News* and a string of other smaller publications, and she had a good undergraduate degree and a very relevant postgraduate degree. That application gave her a job as the production assistant at the *Daily Mail's Ski and Snowboard Magazine*. She was introduced to QuarkXPress and had to set up classified ads. 'I was thrown in at the deep end and spent a few late nights fumbling around,' she says. Emma also had to do picture research, but although she found it very boring, at least it was paid. She earned about £12,500 a year. Emma spent three years working at the *Daily Mail's Ski and Snowboard Magazine*, and after hours in front of the computer every day and some highlights like going to France for a week with clothes, photographers and models, she decided it was time for a change.

Currently she is writing features for the monthly *Kitchens, Bedrooms and Bathrooms Magazine*. Its offices are on the same floor as the ski magazine, and so she jumped at the first and best available position. She started as a sub-editor for the publication, but moved to be a features writer quite quickly. Emma has now worked at the magazine for a year, and she is still enjoying it. 'The best thing about it is that I get to see all the beautiful houses that people have. The worst thing is, well, I can't really think of something there, and that must mean that it's not too bad,' she says and laughs. She is usually shown around the houses by the architects, and often the owners are famous. 'I interviewed Oz Clarke the other month,' she says. Emma is also involved with finding themes and designs for photo shoots, which is often connected with a press launch by big companies such as Habitat and House of Fraser. She is also writing about new products. Some might think that it would be boring to constantly write about interior design, but Emma has not met the wall yet. 'Right now I'm writing about duvets and pillows,' she says and giggles.

She has also kept her connection with the skiing publication, *Where to Ski and Snowboard*, and is working from time to time with the fashion editor. She is helping them in choosing clothing and settings for picture shoots.

The young journalist has no set game plan for her immediate future, but she has certain hopes. She can do one of two things:

either stay in the interior design industry and become an expert there, or broaden her horizons. She definitely wants to go with the latter option, as she does not see herself writing about bed linens for the rest of her career.

The only thing she would like to change about her work is her salary. 'I wish I got paid more, especially when I see what my friends in other professions get,' she says.

Interview by Espen Schiager

Online journalism

- *Internet versions of existing media*
- *Journalism on stand-alone websites*
- *The jobs*

'The website is like a theatre: I love making sure that all the lighting, characters and colours are right each day so that the audience gets the best possible show....Online there's more back-up too, and also more distraction from, the words themselves. It's like writing for the theatre as opposed to writing a novel.'

Tree Elvin, website editor of hellomagazine.com, in an interview with journalism.co.uk, november 2003

Jobs in internet journalism have followed the boom and bust fortunes of the internet itself. At one stage several papers took on scores of journalists to work on their internet sites, only to lay them off later when it appeared that there was no money to be made in that area. Similarly, online publications started up and probably provided good experience for a lot of young journalists, but many of these disappeared pretty quickly.

Because everything happened so fast, it was impossible for anyone to work out how internet publications should operate, and specifically, how they should make their money. No area of journalism stands still for long, but internet journalism whirled around crazily for a while, with jobs there one day and gone the next. It is difficult to foresee exactly how many jobs there will be in the near future, but at least the picture is becoming a little clearer as to what sort of jobs they might be. Some papers, notably *The Guardian* and the *Financial Times*, as well as the BBC, have persevered longer than some of the others, and there are now some good jobs to be had on these and some smaller publications.

Journalism on the internet divides into two areas: the online versions of newspapers, magazines and broadcast media, and the internet-only sites that include some journalistic material.

Internet versions of existing media

The best-known and most successful of these is *Guardian Unlimited* and the BBC's site, which have been in the forefront of internet journalism for several years. In 2003 the *Guardian Unlimited* site had eight million different people visiting it in a month. There are other big sites too, notably ft.com, and Associated Newspapers' thisislondon.co.uk, echoed by thisisgloucester and so on, wherever the Daily Mail and General Trust have regional papers.

When these big sites started up, they generally began as a subbing operation, cutting and pasting material that had appeared in the papers or had been broadcast. All the major websites have changed their appearance radically in the past five years, and at present seem to have settled on quite a busy home page, with lots of boxes advertising the various parts of the site. So the 'front' or home page needs short headlines and single sentences about each story, but when the reader has clicked on the links to get the actual stories, they seem to be getting rather longer. Initially there was a theory that website readers had an even shorter attention span than newspaper readers and stories were kept very short.

As the medium has developed the big players have built teams of reporters working primarily or exclusively for their internet sites. So there are a number of jobs available there, and indeed the subbing and design jobs are increasing too, preparing, for example, single sentence 'internet headlines' for surfers to click on.

The BBC website is the biggest in terms of employment opportunities at the moment. It is a massive operation, employing around 200 journalists writing copy for the site, editing, picture researching, and so on. Almost every internet activity can be found on the BBC site, from hard news, to health advice, to a photo gallery, to a site helping with GCSE revision. And, like BBC broadcasting, it all comes without adverts. If it continues to grow at the rate it has done for the past few years, it will be the nation's biggest news outlet in five years' time.

The BBC site is entirely free and likely to remain so for the foreseeable future. This may not make its rivals at the national newspaper sites and elsewhere very happy: some regard it as unfair competition that the licence fee should be used in this way. Some people criticise the BBC for taking revenue out of the market by providing a free site. Others in the industry feel that the quality of the site raises the profile of internet journalism and raises everyone else's game as well. The BBC's defenders point out that disseminating news, however it is done, fits entirely with the BBC charter. The news dispensed on the internet is, of course, produced vastly more cheaply than is the news for a TV bulletin.

The BBC's online journalists tend often to take the main headline story from the corporation's other services and then provide added value themselves, with analysis and background reporting. The reporters often research and edit the pictures to go with the stories, so they need to be fairly creative and able to think laterally to make a good story package. The newsdesk editors are responsible for building links and monitoring work generally. When the news and features are taken off the site they are all stored in the archive, to which everyone has free access. As well as the reporters and sub-editors, there are a good number of jobs for designers, producing maps and other graphics.

The *Guardian* site employs about 60 journalists. Some work at subbing the material from the paper and getting it on to the site, others write new material specifically for the site, and others have a news editing and copytasting role, assessing stories and deciding where they should live on the site. The site has online-only material as well: for instance, the media section has a 'media monkey diary' which runs new stories throughout the week, not all of which get into the media monkey diary in the following Monday's print version.

The site is free, and likely to remain so, although there are specific services, such as the Wrap and the Informer, which are digests of newspapers, and which are available to subscribers. The crossword, too, is available only to subscribers. By the end of 2003 the *Guardian* site had come close to breaking even. Insiders believe this is because they have not done anything significantly wrong: they haven't been given vast amounts of money to waste, and the whole thing has been grown carefully and with financial rigour.

The jobs, therefore, are similar to those on a newspaper, but a couple of new job titles have emerged both here and in other internet sites. **Uploaders** are those who do shifts (in the evenings for a national morning paper) getting material from the newspaper's electronic queues or baskets on to the internet site. These shifts are usually done by students or graduates who are trying to get into journalism. Uploading is not a real journalistic job, but can be an excellent foot in the door and beats working in a bar.

The term **producer** has also arrived in the world of internet journalism, but it seems to mean a number of different things. It might be someone responsible for bringing all the material together, and having an oversight of the whole operation, perhaps a night editor in print terms. But at some internet enterprises it can mean someone who is researching and developing new areas of the site, or even working on new products, such as text messaging services for mobile phone users. Some internet journalists avoid terms like producer, which they say are an attempt to pretend that the online work is like broadcasting. They say it is still rooted in print journalism, and prefer to use print journalism's titles.

The Times's online operation has a staff of about 35, including some casuals and graphic designers. They do a small amount of reporting, but are mostly organising interactive areas such as 'talking points' with, say, film actors during the London Film Festival. As on the *Guardian* site, the crossword has to be paid for, but unlike *The Guardian*, *The Times* makes readers pay to access the archive. Some nationals now offer a facsimile internet version for those accessing the internet from outside the UK. It is a complete digital representation of every page of the paper, and £90 buys *The Times* and *The Sunday Times* for a year (December 2003 figure). This is an extraordinary bargain: it gets you the complete e-paper, seven days a week, plus the online version and the archive, which is far cheaper than buying the paper, although it's hard to picture anyone ploughing through even half *The Sunday Times* on a computer screen. The papers use a system called geoPoint which tracks where a potential subscriber is dialling in from, so they can arrange that this facsimile version is not available in the UK. All the newspapers seem to be very wary of allowing their online version to interfere in any way with the print version. This is a difficult problem, especially as print circulations are generally dipping slightly.

Some sites also have journalists writing exclusively about film, music and eating out, providing more detailed coverage than can be used in the paper. One of the big things about the internet is that it is so interactive, so there are more jobs on the equivalent of a newspaper's letters sections. All the main sites carry a 'have your own say' area, and a journalist is needed to monitor these contributions, check them for libel and other problems, and also edit them down if necessary.

Journalism on stand-alone websites

This has not turned out, yet at least, to be as fruitful an area for jobs as some commentators had hoped. If magazine buyers are a bit fickle, that is nothing to web-surfers. The people who are happy to pay £3 or more each month for a glossy magazine seem to want to trawl around looking for interesting material on the web, but are certainly not prepared to pay for the privilege of accessing the same site regularly. And the advertisers are not keen, as it is clearly possible to ignore adverts very easily, or indeed arrange for your computer to turn them off.

So plenty of web magazines, those covering women's interest areas, for example, arrived and folded pretty quickly. From the journalistic point of view it seems that what people do on the internet is look at the news headlines, usually through a site associated with a newspaper or broadcasting organisation that they already know and trust. Then they read some item in detail on a subject that interests them. Otherwise, they use the internet to buy things. So the journalism being done on some sites is very close to advertising copy-writing. An example is crocus.co.uk, which has plenty of editorial material but it looks rather basic and it seems likely that the only journalists making much money out of it are Alan Titchmarsh and Charlie Dimmock.

A better bet for a young would-be journalist might be the music websites. There are quite a few of them, including the Yahoo site dotmusic.co.uk and darkerthanblue.co.uk. The bigger ones will pay for freelance articles and might also be a place to try for some work experience. Music reviews, particularly for the small websites, are generally not paid for, but you do get a free ticket to a gig or a club plus the chance to see yourself published. Most websites sell CDs via a link to a retailer, usually amazon.co.uk. The music magazines have websites too, but these are mostly made up of material from the print version. An exception is NME.com, which covers music genres not dealt with in detail in the print version. As with sport, there are a great many young people who would like to listen to rock music all day, write a bit about it and get paid. It is possible to succeed in this area, but only with plenty of determination and hard work.

Another area where journalism has survived the dotcom boom and bust is sport. The biggest presence is the Rivals group, which has become an online microcosm of the magazine industry, including magazines, contract publishing, and unofficial fanzines. Rivals publishes its own successful brand websites, including rivals.net and planet-rugby.com. It has contracts to produce websites for other organisations mounting sporting events, such as the Zurich premiership. Another area of activity is producing pictures, scores and the like for mobile phone companies. Rivals also incorporates around 90 unofficial fanzines associated with various sports and clubs, providing the infrastructure for them to publish on the web. Most of the people writing in this area are amateurs, and the fanzine is a part-time hobby.

Rivals has about 20 journalists, but it is not likely there will be many jobs available in the near future in the UK. Some of the work is being moved to South Africa, where labour is cheaper, and in the days of the internet, it doesn't matter where your terminal is.

Some of the material is used in several areas of the firm's operations: the same material might be on the main website, on one or two of the contract websites, and the first sentence might be whizzing off to mobile phones as well. Some of the journalism involves writing, but the same person would probably source pictures and write headlines, too, so several different skills are involved.

What is not involved, unfortunately, is actually going to a match. It is much more likely that the reporter would quickly write a few snappy paragraphs while watching the TV, to get the story on to the site as soon as possible. There are also decisions to be taken akin to those of a filing editor at an agency: the journalist has to decide which of the various services she will send the story to. The sites may also carry columnists' writings, and in common with others types of internet activity, there is a well-developed interactive element. One of the things sites like this do best is allowing people to have their say, so after an important match they will carry plenty of material emailed in from the public. Rivals seems prepared to carry fairly hard-hitting comments, say about a referee's decision, which the BBC site might be more wary of.

The jobs

Some internet journalism jobs equate directly with a print reporting job: finding something out, probably by talking to someone, and then writing about it. However, most of the jobs seem to combine the skills of a reporter/sub-editor and news editor: the journalist would be doing a bit of research, finding a picture, sorting out material and reorganising it, and writing snappy headlines, or what are known as **teaser text**. This is the equivalent of a **stand-first** or **sell** in a print version: the first sentence or two, in bigger or bolder type, which persuades the reader to have a closer look at the story. Speed is obviously very important, and in that sense the work sounds similar to some agency work. Curiously, accuracy is not as important as in some other areas: if a name or even a score goes up onto a site wrongly, it can be corrected as soon as someone spots it, so it may not be seen as such a crime as getting something wrong in a paper or magazine.

The jobs are reasonably well paid, and might be a useful way into print journalism. However, as the websites become more sophisticated and the people working on them more assertive and confident (their jobs have only existed, after all, for about five years), they may not welcome people who are open about seeing the website work as a stepping stone to something else. So young journalists might need to tread as carefully as they should when discussing their ambitions with older hacks on local papers.

There is disagreement about what might be the best training for this kind of work. Quite a few internet journalists have gone straight into their work from university or from a journalism course, but it seems that the majority at present have come via print journalism. Several colleges and universities have begun online journalism courses, but plenty of people will say that what is required is simply a well-trained or experienced print journalist. All the usual qualities of speed, attention to detail, and the ability to write an arresting few sentences are needed for online journalism, so it seems that there may not be a huge advantage in following a course aimed specifically at online journalism, because that might make it harder to get a print job at the end.

Certainly, it seems clear that a would-be journalist does not need to know too much of the complicated computer technology. You don't need to be a brilliant computer whiz to create a website using Dreamweaver software, so any young student journalist should be able to master that fairly easily if he or she wants to create a website for some sort of student endeavour. But big web operations have, increasingly, developed their own software. And the bigger the organisation you work for, the more sophisticated their software, and the more it will do for you. Someone who is a complete Noddy about computers won't get far, but you don't need a huge amount of computer expertise to get a job in this area.

Liane Katz: online journalist

Liane Katz, who always knew she wanted to be a journalist, was working on the *Guardian* website within a couple of years of completing her degree. She is now chief sub-editor for the politics section of *Guardian Unlimited*, the website for *The Guardian*. She got a job there by applying to them, after finding out that they were recruiting. The fact that she had once completed a work placement there meant she could, according to her, 'talk her way into the job'. She started off as a production assistant, and worked her way up to her current position. After three years working there, she earns £26,300 a year.

The politics section of the website covers UK and sometimes European news, and the journalists working on the site generate their own content. Liane works in a team of four to five people; as well as herself, there is an editor, a political correspondent, a sub editor and one or two reporters. Her job involves processing copy, sub-editing, finding headlines and pictures (*Guardian Unlimited* does not have a picture desk), and generally supervising the whole operation. As they cover rolling news, the work is very fast-paced, which is one of the things Liane enjoys about the job: 'We're very busy, I have to produce accurate subbing very quickly.'

Liane and her team work eight-hour shifts, Monday to Friday. She usually works from 8.30 am to 4.30 pm ('which realistically means 5.30 pm!'), and there is a separate team of night staff, who essentially proof read and carry on working on news content.

Liane said that her work is extremely varied. Subbing on a website is not as limited as subbing on a newspaper, as she gets to carry out more research, work on the layout and contribute ideas in a much smaller team. This is why she prefers being on a website, even though if she was doing the same work for a national newspaper, she might be paid nearly double the amount she gets now. She likes that the fact that it is a young team: the average age is 28, so she feels that the work they do is much more dynamic and exciting.

However, as much as she loves the fast-paced nature of her work, it can also be quite trying. The fact that the news is constantly going up onto the site means that it is rather like agency work. 'You never have a moment free after deadlines, there's always something in your tray or your inbox that you need to be getting on with,' Liane said.

She had always known she wanted to get into journalism as a career, so she started work experience placements early in her life. At 16, she worked for two weeks at *The Guardian*. She won an internship at *The Times* and also spent a few weeks in the summer before university at *BBC World Service*, working on children's programmes.

She completed a BA in History and French at Oxford University, and spent part of that time in Paris, where she freelanced for *The Guardian*. She worked on student radio and wrote a gossipy newsletter occasionally at university, but was not involved a great deal in student journalism. After she graduated, she worked for a dotcom company that dealt with online loyalty programs for internet retailers. She worked in public relations and occasionally in marketing too. Liane said:

'It was a good thing to do, even though I decided I hated it. It was a communicative job, and that helped me.

'I've been really lucky; I've not had to do a postgraduate course or lots of regional work. I've been given lots of opportunity, but I don't think it's necessarily impossible to end up where I have without following a strict career path. It's obviously very competitive, but you have to believe in yourself really. I've known others who've done the same.'

She does not really know where she sees herself in the future. She is happy at *Guardian Unlimited*, but depending on the evolution of the place, she thinks she might be somewhere else in five years' time. 'I might move to another institution that covers online breaking news, or maybe do some travel writing as I've done some before. I want to do slightly more featurey things, with slower deadlines and more editorial input.'

Interview by Syma Tariq

Jem Maidment: text service duty editor

Jem Maidment, a duty editor at Teletext, was planning to go to Lancaster University when he completed his A levels. But a really enjoyable work placement deflected him from university, and he has never looked back.

During the summer of 1992 he was offered work experience at the now defunct *Milton Keynes Gazette*. He decided to delay studying and started working for the paper three days a week writing for the sports pages. Jem has fond memories of his first experience of print journalism and describes the paper as: 'A lovely community paper, independently-owned, that was in an office filled with old newspapers, stained carpets and over-flowing ashtrays.' A traineeship followed the work experience but after a month the paper closed and Jem was made redundant.

However, his writing abilities had caught the attention of his home town's largest paper, the *Milton Keynes Citizen*. In 1994

EMAP, the owner of the *Milton Keynes Citizen* sent the promising young writer on to another of their publications, the *Bedfordshire Times*, where he began his first full time job. Although he enjoyed working on the *Bedfordshire Times*, Jem was forced by personal circumstances to leave the paper. He spent the next two years honing his skills as a freelance and caring for his mother, who had become unwell.

He rejoined EMAP, working at the *Peterborough Evening Telegraph* and taking the NCTJ training course, which he admits he found 'a bit of a nightmare'. He said it was a two-year course condensed into 20 weeks, which covered law, journalism, writing, shorthand, and the production of a weekly paper. After completing his training Jem headed back to Milton Keynes to become deputy editor on a new local Sunday paper. While continuing to freelance for the Sunday paper Jem also dabbled in PR for nightclubs.

In 1998 he began to freelance for the *Hampstead and Highgate Express* and soon moved on to the *Highbury and Islington Express* where in October 1999 he began work as the paper's chief reporter. Being an avid Arsenal fan, Jem found working at the local paper extremely interesting and exciting, as he followed the unfolding story of the club's search for a new stadium. During his time covering the club he became an insider and still occasionally freelances for Arsenal. He wrote many articles about the club and found that the *Highbury and Islington Express* allowed him more freedom to write in-depth pieces than any of the other papers where he had previously worked. '*The High and I* gave me the opportunity to really write.' Jem had previously found the word limitations of other publications he had worked on constricting. During his time on the Islington weekly he also had the chance to report on and investigate Islington Council, which he describes as 'the most amazing in the country'. Islington Council has often hit the national headlines, from the 1980s when it was accused by being part of the 'loony left', to the 1990s as Tony Blair's local council.

Jem is now a duty editor for Teletext where he originally started as a feature writer in June 2001, and where he has also worked as a sub and sports writer. Teletext is owned by the *Daily Mail* group and has hundreds of employees. There are two branches: an interactive information service that can be brought up on home TVs, and the new comprehensive website. They both cover sports, news, finance, entertainment listings, weather and information about holidays.

September 11 meant that Jem found himself writing about the deteriorating international situation, focusing on the war on terror, and in particular, the unfolding events in Afghanistan. Jem regularly interviewed Paddy Ashdown for a weekly column on the war on terror. He has also ghost-written a similar column for former football manager and now commentator Ron Atkinson.

It was, and is, a busy time at Teletext, and Jem enjoys that. He took a leading role in the launch of a new in-house sports section, where he was at the forefront of breaking stories, often before some of the larger news services. It is the excitement of 'rolling news' that enthuses Jem, as well as the fact that Teletext is fundamentally without bias or political affiliations. As duty editor he works long and sometimes irregular hours. He found himself in the office at 2.30 am when the Gulf War broke out and he regularly works 50-hour weeks. Jem decides which will be the lead stories, as well as liaising with the Press Association, which provides Teletext with news.

At the age of 30 Jem earns £32,000 a year. He hopes that the future will bring work on a national daily, although he maintains that the boom in digital news services, of which Teletext is at the forefront, appears to be the way forward. In his present role he doesn't get to write much and says: 'I would love to be writing more in five years, wherever I am and whatever I'm doing.'

Interview by Sam Strickland

5

Agencies

- *The international news agencies*
- *British news agencies*

'With regard to my factual reporting of the events of the war I have made it a principle not to write down the first story that came my way, and not even to be guided by my own general impressions; either I was present myself at the events which I have described or else I heard of them from eye-witnesses whose reports I have checked with as much thoroughness as possible. Not that even so the truth was easy to discover; different eye-witnesses give different accounts of the same events, speaking out of partiality for one side or the other or else from imperfect memories. And it may well be that my history will seem less easy to read because of the absence in it of a romantic element.'

Thucydides, *The Peloponnesian War,*
translated by Rex Warner

A good proportion of the words in many newspapers come from agencies, although this may not be clear from the way the material is presented. Local papers take lifestyle features, recipes, crosswords and the like from agencies, and some of these items appear with a byline which gives the impression that the writer is on the staff. They rely on the fact that few people read more than one local paper. If they did, they might be puzzled to find that 'their' cookery writer appears in papers elsewhere in the country too. In the case of some agencies the material is always credited: every newspaper reader in Britain is familiar with the Reuter credit that appears above or below foreign stories and pictures. In its 150 years the agency has built up a formidable reputation for speed and accuracy.

Agencies produce editorial material, words, photos, graphics, and TV film, which they provide to subscribers, or in the case of smaller regional agencies, which they sell on an ad-hoc basis to newspapers, websites and broadcast stations. The Press Association also has some contracts to provide made-up pages for some subscribers.

There are pluses and minuses to agency work compared with working for a publication. For many journalists, although not all will admit it, part of the fun of their job is seeing their name in print above a story, and if that is very important to you, then an agency may not be the right place to work. Agency reporters do get bylines in papers, but the reporters rarely see them, and they probably do not contribute greatly to their job satisfaction. Staff in bureaux abroad sometimes cut out and send bylined pieces from the papers in their country back to the writer, but by the time they arrive the moment has passed, and it might be in a language the reporter can't read anyway. Agency reporters are more likely to get the buzz from simply being there when, or soon after, the event happened, and beating the opposition agencies by getting a story on to 'the wire' first. Older hacks still talk about the wire, and getting a story onto it, although of course it is all done electronically now. Email means that the wire messages are no longer as puzzling as when William Boot scratched his head over them in Evelyn Waugh's *Scoop*: 'OPPOSITION SPLASHING FRONT-WARD SPEEDLIEST STOP ADEN REPORTED PREPARED WARWISE FLASH FACTS BEAST' or 'COOPERATING BEAST AVOID DUPLICATION BOOT UNNATURAL'.

Another advantage of agency work is simply getting the story done and getting on to the next thing. When covering a breaking story with many developments, the agency reporter writes the story when it first breaks and then writes probably two or three stories every day as events unfold. There is something very satisfying about simply getting a story written quickly, and then writing another one when there is another development. A reporter from a weekly news magazine or a Sunday paper will gather information for several days, and not be able to actually get the story written until just before the deadline. Some agency journalists would find this very frustrating.

The international news agencies

In 4th century BC Greece Thucydides expressed the same concerns that we have today about embedded reporters, Martin Bell's 'journalism of attachment', and the desire to sex up a story: some things never change in the world of journalism. The fact is, though, that the major international agencies still operate in the great tradition of Thucydides: checking facts, trying to be there when something happens, and if not, using several sources to confirm what did happen, and doing their best to get at the real truth.

The long-established major international news agencies are Reuters, whose global headquarters is in London, Agence France-Presse (AFP), which is based in Paris, and the American Associated Press (AP). United Press International (UPI), also American, still exists but has little impact in Britain, either in terms of stories used here or jobs available.

These agencies were all founded in the 19th century, in various quirky ways. Associated Press started when a group of New York newspaper editors wanted to end the practice they had adopted of sending reporters out in rowing boats to meet the transatlantic liners in order to race back to the city with news from Europe. Agence France-Presse acquired its modern name during World War II when several agencies that had been operating outside occupied France merged their operations and some resistance fighters moved into journalism. In 1849 Paul Julius Reuter used carrier pigeons flying between Aachen and Brussels to carry details of stock prices until the telegraph wire between the two cities was installed. The building where the pigeons lived can still be seen in Aachen, with a plaque commemorating Reuter and showing a pigeon. Sadly, it is now a rather scruffy pizza restaurant. Reuter later had a German barony conferred on him and the agency's hacks still talk about 'The Baron' when they mean the company; when buying a round of drinks which they plan to put on expenses, they may say, 'This one's on The Baron.'

There are other agencies based in London reporting back to their headquarters in Australia, Canada and so on, and a foreign national based here might be able to get work experience or even a job on one of these, although there cannot be many opportunities.

The new kid on the block in the agency world is Bloomberg, which appeared from nowhere and within a generation presents a major threat to Reuters with its financial information and services. Bloomberg was founded in 1981 when Mike Bloomberg, who was a general partner with Salomon Brothers, left and used his severance pay to set up Innovative Market Systems. Having been on the other side in the world of financial information, he knew exactly what subscribers needed, and the organisation has expanded rapidly and massively. It now employs 1,600 journalists, and as well as providing subscribers with financial data and news, it has a 24-hour television station and a book publishing arm. Bloomberg himself has gone on to be mayor of New York.

One benefit for many international agency journalists is the greater possibility of foreign travel. It is certainly true that there are more opportunities for travel than in most other journalistic jobs but on the whole, agencies employ people who primarily want to be good reporters, not people who would like to travel the world at someone else's expense and hope perhaps journalism might be the way to achieve that. Half a century ago Reuters was rather like the British Foreign Office: London-based men (they were almost always men) were posted all round the world to report back to London, and thence to the world, on events in the country where they had been sent. This still happens, of course, but there is an increasing emphasis on what is known as 'local hire' where someone who has had the determination to get himself to Vilnius or Kampala is taken on locally to report for the agency. Whereas a couple of generations ago a bureau (the agency term for a reporting office) in Lagos might have had three or four people who had been posted from London, now there might be one or two posted from London, and a couple, either British or Nigerian, who have been employed locally. This is far cheaper for the agency: someone who is posted abroad would get housing expenses, regular flights home, flights to the posting for children, sometimes school fees in Britain paid. A local hire person gets none of this, so foreign postings are very attractive to the employer, less so to the reporter.

Another good thing for reporters working for the big agencies is that they are highly respected as journalists. Agencies report what actually happens, as it happens. The stories have to be **sourced**, that is, it must be perfectly clear to the reader that whatever is being described really did happen. Agencies do not go in for much, if any, speculation and their factual reporting is what makes agency journalists highly prized. The agencies also make tremendous efforts to be impartial, never using, for example, the word terrorist, on the grounds that one person's terrorist is another's freedom fighter. In the 1970s the paramilitaries operating in Belfast were often referred to in Reuter copy as 'urban guerrillas', although I don't recollect those in South Armagh ever being called 'rural guerrillas'.

The journalistic jobs on international news agencies cover all the areas of news production. There will be reporters working either on their own or as part of a team, covering events in a specific country. In cities where the agency has a big operation the reporters will be specialists, often covering a small area of a financial or commodities market. There will be news editors, monitoring what is going on, and checking that everything that needs to be covered has been covered.

The bigger production offices will have teams of sub-editors, going through stories checking facts and polishing the writing. There will be copytasters monitoring the stories that come in, and deciding whether they should be issued. Two further roles that don't appear in newspapers are those of filing editor and possibly slotperson.

The filing editor on any desk is the final arbiter and the buck stops with him or her. The filing editor checks the story one last time, possibly decides which groups of subscribers will want it, and adds computer codes to ensure they receive it. A slotperson in a bureau is the equivalent of news editor, again giving stories a final check before sending them through to head office.

Of course, agency reporters do get out of the office to major events, but increasingly a great deal of work is done on the phone. Financial reporters might get out of the office for a few press conferences and possibly to lunch contacts, but the amount of information they need to produce, and the speed with which they need to get it, means they probably don't get out as much as they would like.

AFP and AP occasionally take on staff in Britain, but there are not enough jobs within these companies to make getting one a serious career plan. Reuters runs a graduate training scheme, for which the competition is extremely fierce. Reuters started as a financial reporting operation, and while this is not so obvious to the general public who see the credits in the papers, financial reporting is still the mainstay of the agency's operation. You are unlikely to get a place on the training scheme without an interest in, and clear ability to learn to report on, the financial world. A real fluency in foreign languages helps too: many trainees are bilingual or have a very good foreign languages degree. Reuters publishes more than eight million words and about a thousand pictures every day, produced by 2,400 journalists in 197 bureaux across the world. But plenty of those journalists are either foreign nationals or have got themselves to a foreign country and then been taken on, rather than getting themselves hired in London and then been sent abroad. To the horror of some older hacks, Reuters has acquired a more corporate air. The advice to would-be graduate trainees talks about customers rather than subscribers, and things like 'client awareness', which might translate as news sense. But all this is probably inevitable, and doesn't alter the fact that it is an excellent training scheme.

There are also plenty of jobs at Bloomberg, and while they don't offer a graduate training scheme, they have been known to take people who have just completed a postgraduate qualification. The pay is very good.

Anyone who does secure a job with these agencies would be well placed on a career path with the agency itself, or to move to a national paper. Dozens of the staff on the broadsheets, and especially the *Financial Times*, started with Reuters.

British news agencies

The main British agency is the Press Association (PA), which provides a complete British news service covering every major event throughout the country. It is not as well known as it ought to be, because papers generally do not credit the agency with stories which they use, and indeed papers have a habit of giving the PA story to a desk reporter, who then makes some changes so the story appears with his or her byline. Sometimes, there is no doubt, the changes are minimal, but the staff person's byline is still there. All major newspapers rely on the PA for back-up coverage of events when they can't get a reporter there themselves, and indeed even when they can: the PA reporter, whose shorthand is almost always the best in any group of reporters, can be relied upon to produce accurate quotes at, say, an important press conference. The PA is also of vital importance to papers at election times, when the agency provides a very fast and accurate results service. It does a similar service with sports results.

The PA has 265 journalists covering everything from courts to politics to sport. There is also a features department, which produces features on anything and everything; these are mainly used by regional papers. The PA runs an excellent training scheme with about 12 places each year, and would be a very good place to start in journalism. The training covers reporting and production for conventional agency services, as well as Teletext and online. However, the PA will take only trainees who have a journalism qualification and have already reached at least 100 words per minute in shorthand. This is because it, like the international agencies, places great emphasis on accurate reporting and note-taking.

Trainees at the PA begin work in Howden, Yorkshire, where the company runs its sport, contract publishing, regional wire, arts and entertainment listings, digital production and TV listings. Trainees then have the chance to move to one of the 27 regional offices the agency has in the UK and Ireland, or eventually to end up in London.

As with the international agencies, subscribers pay a fee for the service and they can then pick and choose which items they want to use, or as is often the case with the national papers, use the PA as a tip-off service, and then research and write their own story.

Dotted about the country there are many other agencies of varying kinds. Some cover courts, and the reporters for these spend all their time, say, at the Old Bailey, or keeping a watch over all the crown courts within a city, and they then sell any interesting or quirky stories to the national papers. A day in court might provide stories for papers in several different nearby towns, and the agency can sell stories in several directions. Newspapers might be unwilling to send a reporter to the court to spend all day waiting for one case.

There are also many regional agencies, with a handful of reporters, covering whatever happens in their area. Big regional and national newspapers have lists of these independent agencies, and if the news editor hears that something has happened, say, in Peterborough, she would get on to the agency to make sure they are going to cover it. Alternatively, the agency reporters hear of something happening in their area, and send the story to the nationals. The stories might be anything from a quirky human interest one, like a local couple coming back from Australia with the England Rugby team and getting their photo taken holding the cup, to some unusual tragedy, to a celebrity story. Agencies use sophisticated software to send their stories to various papers electronically. Similarly, they use software programs to keep track of stories, invoices and payments.

Most of these agencies are fairly small commercial operations, and they are unlikely to have the resources to train someone from scratch. But a student who had completed a fast-track course or a postgraduate diploma might get taken on as a junior. Such agencies make good jumping-off points for the national papers, because if they operate in a newsy area, the young journalist's work will constantly be in front of the national news editors.

Successful agency reporters need to be very creative, scouring all the local newspapers and magazines and constantly seeing angles and possibilities for stories. Agencies often work with photographers, so they can supply a paper with a whole package ready to slot into a page.

Some freelances organise themselves into small agencies, of perhaps only a couple of people, so they can share office space, cover for each other and make other economies of scale. Working for one of the smaller agencies, say with a team of two or three, can be as difficult and stressful as ordinary freelance work. Most agency reporters say they are having to work harder for longer to make a living, that payments from national newspapers have barely risen in the past ten years, and in some cases have dropped. They send their story off, check that it is used, and then find that a story which last year earned £100 earns only £80 now. Because there is no way they could get themselves organised into a central representative body, they have no redress against this. As with freelances, the difficulties of chasing up payments, and the time involved in this, is a constant strain, and agency reporters say they can sometimes wait up to two years for payment. There seems to be no real reason for this, just generally a chapter of accidents: the news desk say they authorised it, but the accounts department can't find it, and so on.

Scott Hussey: agency reporter

Scott Hussey, a reporter at Newsflash agency in Edinburgh, said he feels privileged to meet new people all the time, sometimes at the best, and other times at the worst moment in their lives. He loves the buzz of getting stories at speed, and seeing his stories in print, sometimes in several different papers at once.

Scott studied psychology at Durham University, but realised that it was not what he really wanted to do in life. He then did a postgraduate news journalism course at City University which led him to his real vocation, reporting. Scott admits he is a very nosey person, the sort that wants to know everything that is going on. 'That is very necessary in a journalist,' he said.

His first real journalistic experience was at school, doing reviews for the student paper, which he really enjoyed. At university he did a lot of student journalism because he believes it is very good experience to get to know the way papers and magazines work. While at university and after finishing his degree he did eight weeks' work experience on a number of papers, among them *The Belfast Telegraph, Anglia TV, The Daily Star, The Times* and *The Daily Express*. Scott said he showed that he was a very dedicated journalist and this is why everywhere he went he was taken seriously. His job at *Newsflash* is his first paid job. He is working as one of a team of seven reporters, and is enjoying every minute of it. The agency also has two feature writers and five photographers.

A normal day at work for Scott would be very busy. 'I will come in at eight in the morning, have a look through the papers and then go out in the street and work on a story that the news editor will have assigned to me. It could be a court case, a car crash. We cover everything except sports and politics.' Scott says: 'The best thing is getting to meet new people continuously, sometimes famous. That's very interesting. You meet them at the best time of their lives or perhaps the worst and that for me is a privilege. I am mostly in my office, but when I go out there I truly enjoy it.'

As well as being assigned to stories, the reporters are expected to spot stories themselves, either by careful reading of the papers and thinking about follow-up stories, or perhaps through contacts. Their main customers for stories are the Scottish editions of the national papers, plus the *Daily Record* and some regional dailies. Scott always has to think about pictures when he is following a story, as the agency needs to provide a complete package to its subscribers.

Without hesitating, Scott said that money is the worst bit of his job. 'Money, hours and pressure,' he said. Although he does not get paid very well, Scott does not mind because he is doing what he enjoys. The pressure also mounts up, but this in a way is good, he said, because it gives the journalist more motivation.

The Scottish editions of the national tabloids are relatively generous about giving bylines to agency reporters. Scott says: 'One of the best things about working at an agency is that it is possible to get several bylines in different papers for the same story. On the flip side, you may get no bylines for a story you have put a lot of effort into, and that is frustrating.' Scott said that sometimes if a staff reporter rewrites a story considerably, he doesn't mind if there is no byline, but it is frustrating if the story appears as he wrote it, but with someone else's byline. 'There is a lot of competition in Edinburgh from other agencies and newspaper reporters and it is always rewarding when you do a better job than they do. The buzz of doing well is great, but it is better to be credited for it with a byline!'

As a young journalist, Scott Hussey has still many dreams to fulfil. At present he is happy with what he has achieved, but in the next five years he hopes to be working for a national paper. He advises student journalists to do a lot of work experience, which is the most important bit of a journalism degree. He said that the main things about journalism are learned when doing some work experience. 'There is not much you can be taught, you pick up things and learn as you are doing the work for yourself,' he said. He advises students to start doing their work experience in local papers because they are the best places to learn. 'Academically you can be very good, but that does not matter, what matters is what you do out there in the real world,' he added.

Interview by Pamela Leston

Andrew Tongue, agency sports reporter

When Andrew Tongue first decided to be a journalist, his ambition was to be a foreign correspondent, and after he finished his degree he set off for Azerbaijan. But he is now settled on the sports desk of the Press Association, just completing a three-year traineeship. 'I don't have any interest in becoming a foreign correspondent any more! I have a quite settled lifestyle now and the last thing I want to be doing is dashing off to dangerous places. Maybe I have matured a bit in that respect.'

Andrew loves all sport, from football to rugby league and rugby union, as well as boxing, American football, cricket and athletics.

He enjoys his job, at the PA offices in Howden, Yorkshire, because it is exciting to talk to football and rugby players and managers. At the moment, however, most of the work is not glamorous and involves the routine job of checking if players have injuries and what Conference level club fixtures are on each day.

Before working for the Press Association, Andrew wrote for the London based *Financial News*. The paper focuses on investment banking and economics, which he liked as it enabled him to meet the financial heavyweights of the city. This was his first paid job as a professional journalist, and it gave him good training. He got the job while studying for a postgraduate diploma in newspaper journalism at City University: '*The Financial News* approached the university asking if anyone would be interested in the job, so I went for it.'

Andrew changed from finance to sport because he got very involved in playing sport himself. 'I took up boxing and also played some football. I'm a fitness fanatic, and spend three nights a week in the gym doing mainly weights work. I also run at least two nights a week and cycle.' The PA training has been very varied. The agency's main sports subbing operation is in Howden, with material being processed there from a vast number of games all over Britain and indeed the world.

Andrew has worked on the sport Teletext service, producing copy about the Nationwide League games and has spent time on the international desk, subbing incoming European football and rugby copy. He has also worked on the main sports wire, subbing Premiership match reports and reports from rugby's Zurich Premiership as well as cricket. Andrew enjoys the agency work, and doesn't mind about not getting bylines at the moment. 'A lot of what we do involves rewriting what's on the club websites. I'd feel guilty if I had a byline for that sort of thing. Any really big stories we write we do get bylines on the PA wire, so at least our names are there for all the clients to see.'

All this is a far cry from how he started in journalism when he left Bristol University with a degree in politics. 'After I finished my degree I decided that I wanted to be a foreign correspondent so I packed my bags and went to Azerbaijan without any set plans. My family thought I was mad. When I got there it took a long time to find work but I eventually found an English paper and I began writing on the British oil industry based there. However it didn't really work out for me as there was little stability, so I decided to move back to London where I didn't have to worry about my legs being blown off by a land mine.'

But even in London Andrew found it hard to find work. 'Advice from friends made me realise that to be a journalist you need a postgraduate qualification, so I did the City University postgraduate newspaper diploma.' He added: 'I chose City because of its central London location, its close links with the industry, and its good reputation.'

Interview by Rickin Majithia

6

Charities, NGOs and travel brochures

- *Charities*
- *Travel brochures*

Charities

This chapter gives some idea of the range of jobs that might be said to be nearer the journalistic end of the public relations spectrum. That is, they are as much about writing and editing as they are about public relations (PR). There are obviously a great many other PR jobs, especially in industry, which are more about PR than they are about writing.

The big charities, pressure groups and non-governmental organisations (NGOs) have good opportunities for journalists. There is no set pattern as to how these jobs are organised: in a very small charity the one and only fundraiser might also be the communications officer, responsible for press relations and for producing a newsletter as well. Or the charity may hire a freelance journalist one day a week to produce the newsletter, or it may be done by one of the small design/publishing enterprises (see Chapter 8).

In the huge charities there may be many opportunities for journalism. There will be perhaps a dozen or more people in the PR department, and rather more spread out among many departments, publishing several different newsletters, campaigning brochures, leaflets for service-users, briefings for MPs, and maintaining an extensive website. They may also have what amounts to an in-house journal for the volunteers in the shops. It is impossible to work out how many openings there might be, and what the jobs might be on the bigger charities, as the various publications are often done by different departments, and the design might be done by a department of graphic designers who do not see themselves as journalists at all. Some of the people doing these jobs may not have a conventional journalistic background.

The dozen or so press officers of Cancer Research UK, one of Britain's biggest charities, are divided into three teams. One looks after health issues and campaigns, and is therefore generally dealing with the health correspondents of papers and magazines. Another covers more scientific matters, and generally deals with the science correspondents, and a third team is responsible for PR issues involving celebrities and patrons, organising photo shoots and so on. This team often deals with lifestyle magazines.

About half these press officers come from a conventional journalistic background, and the other half from the specialist science writing and communication courses run at several universities, including Imperial College, London and Bath University.

These jobs might be more creative in the journalistic sense than PR jobs in industry. A PR for a big firm might spend quite a bit of time in crisis management, defending the company's image against adverse publicity, for instance. But PR for a big charity will involve creative campaigning in possibly two areas: to get the charity's name into the press, thereby generating more donations, and to raise public awareness about, say, the dangers of too much sunbathing. A PR for a charity might research a project the charity is involved with, devise a suitable angle, organise a press release and publicity and then have the satisfaction of seeing the idea get into print. It is very similar to being a conventional print journalist, without the final byline.

PR people in big organisations are also sometimes involved in ghost writing opinion pieces for their directors, as indeed PR people in Whitehall ghost articles for ministers. There is obviously satisfaction to be had from writing something and seeing it in print, although it certainly must seem odd to see it under someone else's name, and know that they haven't written it.

The good news with charities and campaigning organisations is that the actual employment arrangements are less random than in some other areas of journalism. The jobs will be advertised, probably either in *The Guardian* or through one of the charity recruitment agencies. There will be a conventional interview procedure, and the pay often compares extremely well with first or second jobs in journalism.

As with newspapers and magazines the jobs are likely to go to someone who has done some volunteering in the charity sector. Volunteering, of course, is simply work experience under another name. Some of the big charities, Cancer UK for example, now run their own training schemes, where graduates get a chance to work in several different areas over a couple of years.

Travel brochures

Travel writing is an enormous and expanding field, and there are freelance and other opportunities here, especially for people who know a particular city well and can produce a chapter or some information for a new guide. At least to start with, this is likely to be a matter of luck: someone working in the tourist industry in Barcelona might get to know someone who is updating one of the guides and be asked to write a chapter. The smaller and more specialised travel companies have brochures with a great deal of editorial material. Simply Travel's brochures, for example, run to 6,000–8,000 words each.

Needless to say the jobs of travelling around the target area and writing the material are highly coveted and not easy to come by. They generally go, not to a conventional journalist, but to someone who is experienced in the travel industry and can write. But once again, there may well be freelance opportunities if one can get to know the right people. Some food guides have food experts eating meals all over the place and producing reports that are then actually written up by a freelance journalist.

Getting into this is likely to be even more a matter of luck than with some other areas. A determined person may succeed, but it is likely to be via a circuitous route. The most likely path would probably be through the travel pages of a newspaper or magazine, and by making plenty of contacts through whom extra freelance work might be found.

Alison Hunter: charity press officer

Alison Hunter, press officer at Scope, the disability charity, was not born with a silver pen in her mouth and a shorthand notepad in her hand. Journalism found her through a friend and charmed her by its versatility and freedom.

She studied for a BA in Sociology at Sheffield University and graduated in 1997. She then took a job teaching English at a local school for six months. She was intrigued when a student friend told her about the postgraduate broadcast journalism course at the London College of Printing (LCP). She joined the course in 1999 and graduated in 2000.

During her time at the LCP, Alison did work experience at the Air FM radio station in Leeds. It was not a pleasant experience as she felt that the commercial station did not have a strong focus on news coverage. She worked in a newsroom with only four staff members and was relieved to move to the more serious news coverage of the BBC.

After gaining her postgraduate diploma, Alison did work experience at the BBC London Live radio station. She started as a broadcast assistant, setting up interviews and working on stories. She was then offered the job full-time and started reporting and preparing material for hosts on the station's breakfast show.

Although working at the BBC was pleasant, Alison wanted to travel. She went to Australia to freelance for Sydney talk radio station 2GB and found it to be quite different from her experiences with the English media. The station's news coverage was obviously based on Australian events and she didn't have any Australian contacts. But the radio station produced many British-themed programmes and she was able to use her contacts back home in Britain.

Her journalism studies were a great advantage when she applied for her current job at Scope, a charity organisation campaigning for civil rights and equality for disabled people with the focus on those with cerebral palsy. The job was advertised in the *Media Guardian*. Scope was looking for someone with a versatile approach to journalism; someone who knew what journalists wanted and needed, who could feed them the right information and get Scope positive media coverage. Alison felt that her academic entry into journalism had taught her this and Scope agreed.

The press officer job at Scope fits her like a glove. She doesn't like the commercial media and always wanted to work for a charity. So she was delighted to get the Scope job, even though she says that getting work at a charity press office is often hard and one can't be too picky. But she says that charity press work was an 'obvious' career for her and she enjoys her freedom to do something different every day.

Her desire for a versatile workday is also met at Scope. She produces video features and submits articles to publishers. Either her articles are printed verbatim and she gets a byline, or her work is rewritten by other journalists to fit their publication. She writes daily press releases, provides media training for young colleagues, manages Scope campaigns and deals with the issues that Scope targets. Her favourite task is creating media strategies, deciding what information should be fed to which publications and broadcasters and maintaining good relations with her press contacts.

So Alison hasn't got any plans to leave any time soon. She doesn't mind the journalistic limits of representing an organisation – she takes pride in doing so and says that this is one of the best benefits of her job, along with the pay, which is better than that of a mid-level journalist. She does, however, regret that she didn't stick with traditional journalism for a bit longer and is pondering a return at some stage.

Interview by Nicolai Hartwig

Caroline Abomeli: charity press assistant

Caroline Abomeli, a recently graduated journalist from London, had to beat 300 other applicants to get her first job, as a press and communications assistant at the Diana, Princess of Wales Memorial Fund. The job was advertised in the *Media Guardian.*

For her, a normal day in the press office starts when she goes through the day's papers, looking for cuttings about the fund. 'I go through my emails, and I send a news digest email to the other employees,' she says. 'In fact, I'm the only one in the office who can burn CDs, so I do that as well at times, and I work on updating the website.'

Caroline realised that she wanted to become a journalist when she was a child. She started doing work experience at the age of 13 at *The Guardian, The Young Telegraph* and her local London newspaper. 'I started to look at press offices as well,' Caroline says. 'I got work experience in Virgin Records and the Metropolitan Police press offices.' She found that while work experience at Virgin Records only meant shadowing the full-time employees, the Met allowed her to do press releases on her own.

Caroline got her work experience, both before and during the time she studied for a BA in Journalism and Contemporary History at City University and Queen Mary, University of London, by sending copies of her CV to all the places she could think of. 'It is very important that you use all the potential contacts you have,' she says. 'For example, I got my work experience at *The Guardian* through a friend's mother.'

Caroline's first paid job, when she was still a student, was as production manager at topcareers.net, a website for graduate jobs. 'It basically meant running round trying to get stories and proof-reading,' she says. 'I got that job accidentally; I originally applied for another one and was offered this one anyway. It was £5 an hour, which was great at the time. They asked me to come back the next summer, and they still phone me up now.'

It was not until her second year as a journalism student that Caroline decided to look at other careers, including press office work. 'I felt as though I was too narrow-minded,' she says. 'I have always wanted to be a journalist, but I couldn't find any jobs I wanted in the *Media Guardian*.' She finds her degree study useful, although she wishes that she had continued working at shorthand until she got a certificate.

Caroline says the best thing about her present job is that it can be very exciting. 'The best thing I have ever done was to coordinate an HIV/AIDS conference,' she says. 'The worst thing about it is that the job can be totally chaotic at times and completely dead at others. It is very ad hoc.'

Caroline's advice to students is that they should keep their options open. 'It is difficult to get a paid job, and that can really knock you down,' she says. 'That's why you should do loads of work experience, even if it's crap. It will still look good on your CV. Keep the contacts you make, and send them cards for their birthdays and for Christmas. Make sure they remember you.'

Caroline also advises students to read the *Media Guardian* to see what skills employers ask for in their adverts.

'I have no idea where I will be workwise in five years' time,' Caroline says. 'All I know is that I want to make £30,000 a year by then!'

Interview by Emma Lundin

7

The Visuals

- *Photojournalism*
- *Picture researchers*
- *Picture editors*
- *Cartoonists*
- *Artists*
- *Graphic and other designers*

'F8 and be there.'

Catchphrase of New York photographer Weegee (Arthur Fellig) in the mid 20th century who called himself Weegee (Ouija), because of his seemingly supernatural ability to be first at a crime scene. Actually it was because he listened, with their agreement, to police radio frequencies.

'There is nothing in the world which does not have a decisive moment.'

Henri Cartier-Bresson, quoting the 17th century French Cardinal de Retz

---

Photojournalism

Most of the illustrations in newspapers and magazines are photographs. A small regional paper will have a couple of photographers who cover everything from car crashes to fashion features. On a national it get highly specialised, with the staff photographers generally covering news and sport, and a wide variety of freelance photographers specialising in everything from fashion, gardening, food to the arts. There are relatively few staff photographers even on national papers – perhaps between 12 and 20, and quite a few of those may well work on a semi-permanent shift arrangement.

More freelances cover news as well, particularly working abroad on wars, coups and disasters. As national newspapers get larger, with ever more sections, there is a need for more and more photos. These come from freelances, picture agencies, and the hundreds of picture libraries. Photographers are often regarded as fairly volatile people who need careful looking after. This is probably true in many cases, and may be something to do with the general stress of the job.

The news photographer

To the outsider, news photographers are among the most glamorous of journalists, getting dramatic shots of a conflict, an earthquake, or a flood. Some of these images resonate down through the generations: young people who were not even born at the time recognise some of the most famous shots from the Vietnam War, or the 1963 Dallas motorcade, or even, from 20 years before that, the World War II shot of the US marines raising the Stars and Stripes at Iwo Jima.

The obvious thing about being a photographer is that you really *do* have to be there. A reporter could, if necessary, make a few phone calls and produce a report on an event even though he or she missed it. Even when reporting a war (although the best reporters would not rely on it), they can at least get some material from one side or the other or both, without being in the war zone themselves. Photographers can't. This means they have the most dangerous jobs, and indeed most journalistic casualties are generally among photographers and camera people.

Few photographers are called upon, or indeed want, to photo-graph war. But every photographer has to be out and about somewhere all the time, travelling often long distances every day to get photos of people and newsworthy events. This means it can be a very stressful job, being constantly on the road, dashing from one event to the next. And there is no going back. If a reporter has missed some vital point, he can probably check it later, either with the people involved, or by consulting a colleague or an agency. But the photographer often only has that one chance to get a good picture, and if he doesn't get it, he faces seeing an agency picture in the paper the next day instead of his. The phrase 'F8 and be there' sums it up. F8 is a fairly obvious aperture setting and the implication of the expression is that the technology isn't that important; being in the right place at the right time, however, is critical. Cartier-Bresson's catchphrase is perhaps a little more subtle, implying as it does that even the most mundane event has a moment worth capturing, and the skill is to find that moment.

A news photographer's day might start in the office, but it is more likely that there will be a phone call late the night before or first thing in the morning with instructions for the first job of the day. If it is quiet, the photographer just might turn up in the office later to touch base with the picture editor, but since pictures can now be emailed in, it is very likely that a photographer will not appear in the office for weeks. It may be that the only time the whole picture team of a national paper will get together will be at the Christmas party.

So the job of a photographer can be a bit lonely and lacking in the comradeship that there would be in a newswriting operation. There is a different comradeship with the rivals from other papers, however, and it seems that a staff photographer now sees much more of rivals than colleagues.

Given the constant travelling needed for the job, it is no surprise that most news photographers are fairly young. As they get older many of them prefer to do more desk work, becoming picture editors, perhaps. Others opt for a slightly easier life, moving into photography for books, magazines, brochures or company reports. Many photographers combine some of these different areas, taking news pictures part of the week, thus keeping their byline before the public, and then doing more lucrative work, perhaps brochures for City firms, on other days.

Local newspaper photographers dash around their area all week, covering several different events each day. Most of the illustrations in local papers come from their own photographers: it is unlikely that a local paper would be prepared to pay agency fees, and in any case, when covering a smaller area, it is possible for photographers to get most of the pictures the paper needs.

On a national, however, it is likely that a much larger proportion of the pictures will come from agencies or freelances operating wherever the news event is happening. It simply would not be feasible to send a staff photographer to, say, Newcastle for a one-off picture, unless it were for a very important event. The introduction over the past few years of electronic picture transfer has made getting pictures from freelances much easier. It is a gripe among some national newspaper photographers than they never get outside the M25 nowadays, and there is probably some truth in that. But the fact is that the papers, with their dozens of pictures, are almost entirely compiled on the day so it is simply not worth sending a staff photographer too far afield. The exception is at elections, when it is usual for photographers to follow party leaders and others around the country, and one-off national or international events such as President Bush's visit to Britain in 2003.

Photographers have large amounts of expensive equipment, which needs constantly updating. Usually staff photographers get an allowance to cover this, but the actual equipment belongs to them. Similarly, they probably have to have a car to get around; staff photographers may have company cars, or else they will receive an allowance to help cover their motoring costs.

Computers have changed all aspects of journalism dramatically, but nowhere is this more so than with news pictures. Just a few years ago, photographers had to return to the office to print up their photos in a dark room and these were then scanned into the system to go into the pages. If they were too far from the office, photographers would have had a mobile dark room in the back of the car, and would be fiddling around developing film with chemicals in a black bag. All this has gone. The photographer takes the photo with a digital camera, downloads the photos directly into a laptop, chooses the best ones, possibly edits or crops them a bit, and then emails them into the office via a mobile phone link. At least this part of the job is now easier, and there is not the constant pressure there used to be to get the material back to the office in time. But the downside is that the photographers miss out on the interaction with picture editors, looking at the prints, discussing which is the best shot, and perhaps getting a bit of a pat on the back.

Magazine photographers

The vast majority of photos in magazines are taken by freelances. The photographers who do fashion shoots for the glossies are well-paid, high-profile people, many of whom have become celebrities themselves, even household names, helped in some cases by marrying supermodels. A top fashion photographer is in another world compared to a national newspaper photographer: fashion photographers have assistants, studios and, of course, extremely expensive equipment. These photographers often get commissions in 'spin-off' areas as well, including posters and books.

The photographers who take the brilliant photos of gardens for glossy magazines such as *Country Life*, for example, almost always get involved in photography for some of the many highly illustrated gardening books. On glossy magazines the features can sometimes be almost entirely picture-led: a freelance submits a set of pictures of a beautiful garden, the art editor likes them and so a feature writer is commissioned to provide some words.

Similarly, there are specialised food photographers, who also work with assistants, set designers, and home economists who actually prepare the food and make it look mouthwatering.

Sometimes these picture-led features are based on a newly published book. The publishers may have struck a deal with a magazine to use some of the material as a feature, in exchange for a line or two about the book.

Arts photographers take photos for the arts pages of the papers, but also sell their work for CD covers or opera company brochures and programmes.

Digital photography has arrived for most pictures in newspapers and many magazines. But when the photos are the main point of the feature, large-size transparencies are still used and are scanned in, because this gives a better quality. This may change in the near future, however, as the technology for digital photography is improving all the time.

How to get into press photography

Photographers get into the job in a similar way to reporters, usually with a training course, work experience and then employment on a local or regional paper or magazine. To get onto a national, it is a matter of getting shift work, either during holidays, or by giving up the staff job in the provinces, moving to London, and hoping to set up enough shifts to keep going until a staff job comes up.

For a photographer trying to get a new job, the portfolio is even more important than the cuttings file for a reporter. Securing an appointment with art and picture editors to show them the portfolio is simply the only way to proceed. From there the photographer hopes that the editor might consider using some pictures she has already taken, or be so impressed with her ability that she would be commissioned to cover something.

The best-known and most successful press photography course is at Sheffield College, which runs NCTJ-accredited press photography and photojournalism courses. The course takes a variety of students, with or without degrees. There are also respected courses in photojournalism at the London College of Printing.

There are many other courses on photography at all levels, but it would be important for someone interested in press photography to check just how much of a course is devoted to press photography.

Nick Morrish: trainee photographer

Four months into the photography course at the Norton Centre in Sheffield, Nick Morrish landed a staff job with the *South Wales Argus*. He plans to complete the course, returning to Sheffield to finish assignments and take the NCTJ preliminary exams. 'As far as getting into press photography in this country, the Sheffield course is the industry standard,' says Nick. The tutors encourage students to apply for jobs when they come up, indeed papers regularly contact the course tutors asking about likely candidates. And students who are offered jobs are encouraged to take them, and complete the course while working.

Nick did a four-year degree in American History at the University of Kent, and as part of his degree, spent a year at Penn State University in Pennsylvania. He had always been interested in photography, but it was here that his hobby became a passion, when he started taking pictures for the student newspaper, the *Daily Collegian*.

This daily paper, free on the campus, is a massive operation, with 200 people working for it. Most of these are students volunteering, but there are a few paid staff. Nick generally did two or three assignments for the paper every week, and admitted that sometimes he was spending more time on the photography than on his studies. By the end of his time there he had had 60 pictures published in the paper. There were so many editions with his byline that he had to FedEx them home while he spent some time travelling.

Meanwhile, he was building up a portfolio with a range of as many different types of photograph as possible, and he also worked in a camera shop after he got back to his home in Cardiff.

When he returned to Canterbury to complete his final year Nick went along to the student newspaper there. But after the bustle and professionalism of the set-up in the US, he found the student paper back home was too amateurish. So he concentrated on finishing his degree and taking photos when he could to improve his portfolio.

After Nick graduated in 2002 he worked in a photographic laboratory, and continued to take photographs for his portfolio. He feels that a turning point came when there was a mountain fire near his home in South Wales. 'I went to the fire, took some pictures and there was one in there that was a winner. The local weekly took it and it was published, and things took off from there. 'I began talking to editors and finding out about courses. I applied to Sheffield and never looked back really.'

A spell of work experience at the *Western Mail* in Cardiff also helped to give him an insight into the professional world before he set off for the course in Sheffield.

The South Wales Argus, a three-edition evening paper based in Newport, has a team of seven photographers. They work shifts, the earliest starting at 8 am. Nick has a company car, which is essential for the job: in his first full month he drove 1,500 miles for work.

He says the best thing about the job is meeting so many different people. 'You don't just go into an office and stay there until it is time to go home. You get out and get to do so much different stuff. Also there is the point that you are documenting a historic moment.'

Another thing he likes is that photographers have to think on their feet all the time. 'You are constantly trying to get something different, to make something ordinary look extraordinary,' he says.

And the worst thing about the job? 'There isn't anything,' says Nick.

Like every photographer, Nick is constantly adding to his portfolio whenever he gets a really good new picture. He will have exams to take when he completes his training in a year or two, in newspaper practice and law, and photographic practice as well as actual photography. Then he thinks he might want to try his luck in Dublin, elsewhere in Europe, or perhaps he might head back to the United States.

Picture researchers

As newspapers grow bigger and magazines proliferate, picture research has become a growth area. It would be impossible for staff photographers to produce a small fraction of the pictures needed to fill, say, *The Sunday Times*, each week. So pictures must be sourced elsewhere. Some will arrive via the major agencies, and these all need to be assessed and shortlisted for possible use. But many will have to be found either by searching the publication's own picture library, by searching the various picture agencies, which mostly have online photo libraries, by contacting photographers to find out if they have the right thing in their own library, or by commissioning freelances. Newspapers and magazines have become ever more inventive about their illustrations, and use all sorts of slightly random things like early woodcuts, old drawings and prints to illustrate different features. A national newspaper will have around 30 or 40 picture editors and researchers who organise the vast number of pictures needed for all the different sections. There are more than 700 libraries supplying pictures fairly regularly to national newspapers, many specialising in particular areas, such as rock music, or food, for example. The best known is Getty Images, which has become the market leader, after swallowing up several smaller picture libraries. About 200 of these libraries have online catalogues, so the researcher can view the pictures on screen, and then choose the right one. In most cases the researcher will provide a dozen or more possible pictures, and the page designer will make the final choice. For those libraries without online catalogues, there will be emails going backwards and forwards, and the library will email low-resolution images from which the final choice can be made.

With so many pictures to choose from, the picture researcher's job is a new area in which newspapers can be competitive. The choice of pictures has multiplied many thousand-fold in the past few years, so the researcher needs plenty of visual skills to make sure she selects the best ones. Whereas until recently the researcher would spend a lot of time waiting for couriers to arrive with prints, now she can be more proactive, searching and choosing images electronically via the internet. Photographs can often be paid for over the internet and downloaded directly, which saves time. Big picture libraries usually have electronic systems for generating invoices for their orders.

Picture researchers will also contact other papers and some-times agree a fee for using something another newspaper has already got. As well as tracking down pictures, researchers are also likely to find themselves commissioning freelances and liaising with staff photographers.

Fashion and interior design magazines will obviously use new pictures for all their main features, and, indeed, the picture is often the whole point of the spread. But they too have researchers to call in pictures to illustrate small items, such as gardening columns or recipes.

As deadlines approach, even on monthly magazines, the picture researcher's job can be come quite stressful and involve long hours. And on national dailies it involves shiftwork, as someone has to be there late to assess any agency material than comes in, and find more pictures to illustrate late-breaking stories.

How to become a picture researcher
There is no standard career path for getting into picture research. Many picture researchers have a degree or other qualification in

photography, but they might also have come to the job via a news-desk or picture desk assistant role. They might have worked in the dark room in the days when newspapers had them, or have started work in a picture library and then moved across. On specialist magazines the picture researcher's role is much less complicated: on a gardening magazine, for instance, she would need to be familiar only with the various garden picture libraries and free-lances specialising in this area. But on a national newspaper there are so many different possibilities that a researcher would almost certainly need quite a lot of training when first starting the job.

Picture editors

Some picture editors are former photographers or picture researchers; others were senior journalists who had an eye for, and interest in, photography. On a newspaper the picture editor assigns photographers to cover stories, produces a picture list for the editorial conference, makes sure the work gets done in time, and if he or she is a good picture editor, as with any other leader, concentrates on getting the best performance possible out of the team. A national newspaper receives an average of 3,000 images a day of live news and sport from staff photographers and agencies. It would be impossible for the picture editor to assess all of them, so a team of deputies goes through some of them to make sure no brilliant image is overlooked.

A major task is to find striking images suitable for the front page. In most newspapers the editor and one or two other senior executives will make the final decision on the front page picture, but it is up to the picture editor to select several pictures for consideration, and to ensure that a good agency or freelance picture has not been overlooked.

A small weekly paper is unlikely to have a picture editor: the editor and or news editor would commission photographers and choose the pictures for the various pages. The most senior photographer may have some of the responsibility of a picture editor, discussing and helping to choose the pictures for the front and the main news pages. As with the news on a local paper, most of what is available is used in the paper, so it is not a case of selecting from thousands of available images, but more of making sure there are enough to fill the pages.

Cartoonists

> 'It's not an exalted art form. It's lonely, low, scurrilous and
> rude. It's supposed to be. But I think you can be serious at
> the same time as the piss-taking. There is a serious point
> buried in there, somewhere. But the point is also to make
> people laugh and the best ones are when you do both,
> when you hit the spot and make people laugh.'
>
> Steve Bell of *The Guardian*, interviewed by *3AM Magazine*

All the major regional and national papers have cartoonists, mostly working on a contract arrangement. The contracts will vary considerably, some cartoonists being paid for a certain number of drawings each week or month, others being paid a day rate which may involve them in drawing just one cartoon one day, and several another day.

The main types of cartoon are pocket cartoons, political cartoons, strips and caricatures. **Pocket cartoons** are the small single-column jokes which appear on the front of papers, and sometimes elsewhere inside too. Because they are so small they are usually simple line drawings, with a very short caption. They are generally a topical joke. The best known are probably Matt in The *Daily Telegraph* and Pugh in *The Times*. Sometimes these types of cartoon appear inside as well, perhaps in the diary column or other regular feature. **Political cartoons** are generally larger, incorporating elements of caricature, and these generally appear on the comment pages. The best known here are Steve Bell in *The Guardian* and Peter Brookes in *The Times*. One of Bell's best-known is the *If. . .* series from *Private Eye*, and Brookes has developed the *Nature Notes* series which depicts political leaders and celebs as various types of hitherto unheard-of wildlife. Both these cartoonists have become so popular that collections of their work have been published as books. It was Steve Bell who created the peculiar and lasting image of John Major with his underpants worn over his trousers in a parody of a Superman figure. This image was revived with an odd frisson five years after Major lost power, when Edwina Currie revealed they had been lovers and described him as the man in the blue underpants.

Strip cartoons may be politically based as well, or may cover more general current trends. Strips tend to come and go, either because the cartoonists themselves get bored with them, or more likely, because most strip cartoons are very much themed on a particular topical subject or preoccupation, and once that becomes outdated, so does the strip. One of the great survivors is Alex, the cynical and manipulative businessman who appeared initially in the short-lived *London Daily News* and then on the business pages of *The Independent*. Alex was then was poached to *The Daily Telegraph* business section when his creators, Charles Peattie and Russell Taylor were offered a better contract there. But it is odd, and surely against the ideals of cartoonists, that *Alex* cartoons are appearing in adverts for Eurostar. The longest surviving strip must be *Doonesbury*, the US political strip created by Garry Trudeau in 1970 and now syndicated in 1,400 papers across the world, including *The Guardian*.

Some cartoonists develop a character, or even a small cast of characters: Carl Giles, who drew cartoons for 50 years for the *Express* papers, was in a class of his own. His dreadful family, with the battleaxe Grandma, the feeble Vera and all the rest, took on a life of their own, and appeared in dozens of books. He also repro-duced them for Christmas cards and in other ways for charity.

There are many other famous cartoon creations. The scantily clad political ingénue Varoomshka, by the late John Kent, appeared in *The Guardian*, to the fury of some of the feminists on the paper. Simon Stringalong, the smart media type portrayed by Mark (Marc) Boxer in *The Times* in the 1960s and 1970s, was based on reporter Nicholas Tomalin (see Chapter 1).

A slightly different kind of illustration is the **caricature**, and the best-known contemporary creator of these is Gerald Scarfe, whose instantly recognisable style depicts political figures as extremely ugly and sometimes scary. Work like this often accompanies Sunday paper profiles of people in the news. Caricatures are also regularly used in political weeklies.

A few cartoonists work on the newspaper's editorial floor, discussing political and other new developments, and submitting several ideas to the editor or to the back bench. Most, however, work at home, sending material in via email or fax, so cartooning may be a slightly solitary existence, as Steve Bell suggests above. Top cartoonists are very well paid: the best ones earn the same amount as the highest-paid journalists on the paper. Their salaries are helped if they win an award, and may be improved further if another paper, as often happens, tries to poach them. There is a big market for cartoons in the well-known weeklies such as *The Spectator, New Statesman*, and the fortnightly *Private Eye*, and plenty of other magazines also carry cartoons and humorous drawings. Some cartoonists have a contract to produce a strip regularly, others simply send in work, some topical, some less so, on a freelance basis. There is also a lucrative sideline in selling originals, of which most cartoonists retain the copyright, and the galleries in London that sell cartoons have helped provide a good market. As papers and magazines expand, the market for cartoons is likely to increase further, although it is unlikely ever to be an easy profession in which to succeed.

Other types of drawing

As they expand, newspapers and magazines constantly search for new possibilities in illustration, so there are other outlets for artists. As cameras are not allowed in courts and other official inquiries, there is a market for artists who can make sketches of court scenes from memory. There are also opportunities for artists to get drawings published in other areas, perhaps of plants or flowers on gardening pages, or sketches on fashion or arts pages. At one stage *The Independent* regularly used beautiful highly original drawings by Michael Daley.

Graphic and other designers

> Editor (inspecting layout): 'Nice. But there's 800 words of overmatter.'
> Art director: 'The subs can fix that.'
> Ed: 'Can't you just make that picture smaller and why is there no copy on the first page?'
> Art (in condescending voice): 'That is Creative White Space.'
>
> Scenario described by columnist and former editor Janice Turner, *Press Gazette*, May 2003.

Everyone who has spent any time on magazines will know about the tension, creative or otherwise, between the art director and the editor or features editor. For a glossy, the appearance of the pages, and the pictures and other illustrations, are more important than the words. This is why the art department is so important and so powerful.

There has been an increase in the number of people with a background in graphic design who are now working for magazines and newspapers, and this is a growth area for careers. Far more effort is now put into design in every area of publishing compared to a generation ago. Nowhere is this more apparent than in newspapers, where design teams have come into existence in the past 20 or 30 years and have grown steadily in size. You only have to look at the front page of a newspaper from just 20 years ago to see how much more thought goes into design now.

There are those, however, who have arrived in design via a reporting/sub-editing route, and think that the growth of graphic design in journalistic enterprises is not a totally good thing. There is a feeling that sometimes the design is seen as more important than the words, which goes against the whole ethos of journalism, which should be telling people things, not necessarily making something that looks pretty.

However, whether we like it or not, the glossier and more picture-led a magazine is, the more powerful is its **art editor** or

director. This senior person is responsible for all the illustrations and the general design of the whole magazine. No one seems to know why these people are called art editors, when they are not actually dealing with art. The name possibly relates to a time when magazines had far more drawings than photographs. At any rate, the art editor probably has a qualification in design, and has the final say over the choice of pictures, the design and layout of the magazine. The front cover is designed in co-operation with the editor, and possibly the fashion editor, too, but only after a great deal of time has been spent in deliberation.

Much effort is involved in selecting the right pictures. With fashion, for example, merchandise has to be called in, and photographers, stylists, and of course, models have to be booked. Locations need to be researched, or sets built. On a big glossy the art director will have a team of perhaps four of five designers. This may not seem all that many, but it is quite a large proportion, given that the total on the staff of a glossy (excluding freelances) might be only about 30 or 40 people.

In comparison to writing journalists, there are still not that many jobs, perhaps between 20 or 30 on a national newspaper which has a staff of 600 or so writing and production journalists. However, it is a challenging and rewarding area for designers to get into.

The design department at *The Times* has about 14 people involved in page design, working mainly on the features pages. They build many of the features pages, working with the production team on the look of the pages, the position of headlines, editorial, graphics and pictures. They may also be involved in picture selection. There is a big training element in their work, too. There are not enough designers for them to be responsible for all the news pages, but they work with the back bench and layout subs to improve the design of all the news pages, too. The designers are also involved in one-off handbooks, such as those produced for major sporting events.

Then there are about another ten people involved in graphics, producing maps, diagrams and illustrations for use throughout the paper. These range from fairly simple maps, to three-dimensional cut-away pictures of, say, the inside of an aircraft. Then there are the more jokey illustrations, which are almost cartoon-like, and often used to embellish some lifestyle story about consumer spending or suchlike. At present *The Times* is particularly keen on using graphic illustrations on the business pages. The business pages of broadsheet papers are likely to be filled with news about mergers, take-over bids, new business leaders and the like. As these news items are basically the doings of men in suits, any news pictures illustrating these events are likely to be pictures of men in suits. So there is currently a vogue for clever colour illustrations that are a cross between a cartoon, a drawing and a graphic to illustrate some City event such as a merger or takeover battle.

Amber Burrows: graphic designer

Amber Burrows landed a dream job as a graphic designer for *The Times* within a year of graduating. But she first did six months of unpaid work experience with OgilvyInteractive, the web arm of the advertising agency.

Amber studied multimedia design at Northumbria University and graduated in 2002. The course included design for print, web, CD Rom and video. Amber, who did A levels in Art and Design, English and Economics, won the place at Northumbria after an interview when she showed her portfolio. 'I was quite computer illiterate at that time,' she admits 'and my portfolio consisted of paintings, drawings and sketches.'

Now she is fully occupied with computer design at work, and even does some in her spare time. Using a Mac at home she has been designing a website for her father's business and she enjoys making personalised birthday cards for friends.

When she had finished her degree Amber started work experience at Ogilvy Interactive, where they paid expenses, but she had to work in a bar in the evenings to keep solvent. Meanwhile, she kept in touch with the design team at *The Times*, where she had done work experience during her second year at university. And after six months at Ogilvy Interactive, she heard that there was work going at *The Times* so she was able to start paid work there. At first she was doing shifts, as is often the case on newspapers, but after about a year she got a staff job, earning £30,000 a year.

Her main work is designing pages for T2, the tabloid feature section, and much of it involves designing the fashion pages. She designs the pages using Hermes, News International's software which is similar to QuarkXPress. She is given a rough word count of the editorial material, and from this she can work out how many lines of copy there will be. She is usually provided with the pictures, but sometimes she needs to do extra picture research to source more material for her pages. Features sub-editors deal with the words on the pages, Amber's role is to produce the best possible overall design.

'Images and graphics are as important as the copy,' she says. 'If something is badly designed, whether it be a book, website, or newspaper, it is not going to be successful. The world is very competitive, and a paper such as *The Times* has to be easy to navigate and have a consistent style – whether that be colour, type style, rules etc, or the public will go elsewhere, and simply pick up a different paper.'

Amber is one of about 40 designers at *The Times*. From time to time they move around the various departments to gain experience. The number of designers on the paper increased in 2003–4 because of new sections being added, especially on Saturday, and because of the new compact edition.

She works fairly normal office hours, starting at 10 in the morning. The pages for the next day's paper have to be finished by 1.30 pm, so after lunch she begins work on pages for later in the week, or early the following week. There is a team of about five designers doing similar work. She works about one Sunday in a month, preparing pages for the following day. She is very happy in her job: 'I like to be creative myself, and I really like the people here. It is quite chilled out.'

Of her fellow students from Northumbria, few took the same route as Amber. One of the projects on the course was to redesign a broadsheet newspaper and Amber found this fun, but it formed only a relatively small part of the course. Most of the other students went into web design or graphic design for brochures.

She sees herself staying at *The Times* for the foreseeable future, and can happily picture herself doing a similar job in five years' time. Amber is also excited by the possibility of working in New York: a colleague recently did a job swap with a designer on a News Corporation title there and she hopes to be able to arrange something similar at some stage.

Training

Most cartoonists, but not all, will have an art qualification. But the main attribute is a passion for drawing, and, as with every other type of journalism, persistence and determination. Most people involved in design on papers and magazines will now have a degree in graphic design. As this is a growth area there are plenty of courses, but if your interest is in design for magazines or newspapers, it is important to make sure the course you apply for has plenty of work in that area. As the magazine market is predicted to grow a little over the next few years, the number of jobs for graphic designers is likely to grow too.

The normal route to a career in design would be to complete an art foundation course, and then eventually to specialise in illustration and design. Other possible jobs would be in book publishing and working in designing travel brochures and the like. There are also good opportunities for freelancing in this area, and these are discussed in Chapter eight.

8

Freelancing

- *What qualities do freelances need?*
- *What is the job like?*
- *How to get into it*
- *Freelance design*

The idea of being a freelance seems immensely attractive to many people who contemplate a career in journalism – a sort of James Bond of journalism, with the freedom to decide what to write about next, jumping on a plane here, meeting a glamorous celeb there, and composing well-crafted and terse dispatches to a grateful public from time to time.

The reality may not be quite like that. Indeed, those freelances at the top in terms of salaries are freelances because they choose to be, but very many at the bottom are struggling freelances who know they would be better off with a staff job. The James Bond freelances at the top of the tree are constantly in demand so they can practically set their own fees, with commissioning editors happy to let them write almost what they like. Such journalists would not want to be tied down to a particular publication and a regular salary. In many cases the highest paid can command large fees for their journalism because they have made a name for themselves in other areas – Martin Amis and John Mortimer are examples of this. Anne Robinson started as a hack before becoming a TV celebrity, but the two areas of her career began to feed off each other.

At the bottom of the tree there are hundreds of freelances, who may be freelancing not out of choice, but because they have not yet, or may never, secure a staff job. It is extremely hard at the outset to make a career out of freelancing. A young student or graduate will probably not have enough contacts, or simply enough knowledge about how the journalistic world works, to earn a reasonable living by selling articles. A far better bet is to get into some offices doing shifts, and then regard the freelance work as extra money. If it goes well, then gradually the freelance operation might take over. But at that stage it is more likely that the contract and shift work would take over.

Freelances have a better chance of a steady income if they have previously had a staff job. They have then made contacts, learned a great deal about what exactly is needed to be a freelance, and indeed have a good knowledge of the field they want to freelance in.

There are plenty of journalists, especially in London, operating as freelances and working shifts. These people arrange shifts, mostly on newspapers, either by asking for them, or if they are well established, being offered them. Some of them like the freedom this gives, say, for taking time off when they want it. Most are probably doing it in the hope of getting a contract or staff job eventually. But some do a couple of regular shifts each week because it suits their child-care arrangements, or because they spend the other day or two writing freelance features.

What qualities do freelances need?

Freelances need all the usual journalistic attributes (see Chapter 1), but they also need extra bucketfuls of persistence and deter-mination. They must be even better organised than the average journalist. They need to be very methodical about keeping careful track of their work: which ideas they have put up to whom, when they pitched the idea, and the name and title of the person they pitched it to. A freelance is, in a way, his own features editor, office manager, secretary, and sub-editor, and he needs to be well organised to cover all these roles.

If this is going to be the main income, a freelance needs to be very careful about how much work is put in for a particular feature. When agreeing a fee it is important to try to assess how long it will take to write the piece and how much expense will be involved. Publications will generally pay reasonable expenses, so long as this point has been agreed in advance.

Freelances need to be extremely good at juggling work. If things go well, there may be several commissions to complete in one week, and the freelance dares not turn any of them down, in case there are none next week. It is common to accept a poorly paid commission, only to find that a better one is agreed the next day, and they both need to be done quickly. Success depends on being able to get down to both of them quickly, and hope to recover and get the washing and shopping done next week.

Adding to the stress is the constant wait for cheques or money transfers. Publications sometimes lose invoices, forget to pay, don't pay the previously agreed amount and so on. A freelance needs to keep careful records to track payments and to be able to chase unpaid invoices. Many freelances say this continual pursuit of payment is the most stressful part of the job. Successful freelances need to have the determination and persistence to cope with this.

What is the job like?

There are pluses and minuses to freelancing, and the communications revolution has undoubtedly added to the pluses. It is possible to be completely in touch with an office without the hassle of commuting, thanks to email and mobile phones. Well-organised freelances can plan their lives to a certain extent, and do not have to stick to office hours. They can work in the garden on a laptop on a nice day, work late one night if a piece is going well, and then go to the gym in the morning. They can email pieces by the agreed deadline without the worry of post, faxes or copytakers. Another huge advantage for freelances has been the amount of information on the internet. Previously, research often meant trailing off to a government office to collect a report, which can now be downloaded from the internet. Years ago a freelance would have been hampered by not having regular access to the publication's cuttings library, but again, this is much less of a problem now.

The internet has made keeping on top of a complex subject much easier for freelances. But the minuses to freelancing are still the same: the good things about office life are missing, such as the camaraderie and the chit-chat, and the ease of bouncing ideas off colleagues. The solitary nature of freelance work is usually the first of the most regularly cited downsides. The second is the fact that publications are so slow to pay up. Another disadvantage, of course, is that the freelance lacks the pension, sickness benefits and other perks that salaried people get.

The most successful freelances are generally feature writers. They work in a combination of two ways. In most cases they probably **pitch** one or more feature ideas to a commissioning editor or other contact on a paper or magazine. Nowadays, this is usually done by email. If the freelance is already known at the publication, and has got work into the magazine before, it will obviously be far easier. For lengthy features the freelance would probably put in one idea at a time. In other cases, it is probably a good idea to put in three or four ideas, in the hope that the editor will agree to a couple of them.

A successful freelance, like a good specialist reporter, has a long list of ideas, stored in at least two places – in the computer, the personal organiser, or diary. On the noticeboard or in a folder will be lots of cuttings that back up the list of ideas. This list will be regularly updated with new ideas, new angles to existing ideas and so on. This list of ideas shortens itself all too often as the same ideas appear in other publications, or worse, in the publication to which she was about to pitch them. Freelances scour local papers and obscure magazines, listen to local radio, and of course, talk to everyone they meet to try to generate more ideas.

Young journalists are often very concerned that the ideas they put in might be poached. This clearly does happen occasionally, and certainly a freelance with a really good piece of celebrity gossip, for example, would be well advised to negotiate a tip-off fee before divulging it. But in practice genuine features ideas are probably not stolen all that often. The better the idea, and the more suited to the publication, the more likely it is that the commissioning editor will have simultaneously thought of it herself, or that another freelance may have offered it.

When the commissioning editor has looked at the ideas, there will probably be a phone call or email, and the length, scope and angle of the feature will be agreed. For most freelances, publications will have a fairly fixed scale of fees, and it is only when the freelance has become very well known or in great demand that she would be able to negotiate a higher fee. A deadline will also be agreed, and work can begin.

Another possible scenario is that the features team on the magazine decide they want a feature on a particular topic, and approach the freelance to cover it. This probably does not happen as often as the average freelance would like. A constant and consistent moan from commissioning and features editors is that freelances do not prepare their pitches carefully enough. Stories abound of people pitching, say, record reviews to a magazine that simply doesn't use such pieces. The message is: read the target publication regularly and thoroughly. Make sure the idea you are offering would fit exactly into the newspaper or magazine, both in content and style. A successful freelance tailors his work so that the editor on the receiving end can immediately see that it is appropriate for her paper. Of course the constant moan from the other side is that the commissioning editor simply didn't give the idea proper consideration, and obviously that does happen sometimes.

A third way to try to get something into a publication is to send it in 'on spec'. The bigger and better known the publication the less successful this is likely to be. A national newspaper, for instance, would have a team of staff writers, and a huge bank of regular freelances, so a feature arriving from someone they have never heard of will not be considered very carefully. On the other hand, small specialist magazines are probably far more likely to accept something sent in on spec, especially if the writer is clearly knowledgeable.

A freelance might have an idea for a regular column of some sort, and might be lucky enough to get into the office to make a really good pitch for it. A regular column is every freelance's dream, although the paper or magazine might drop the column overnight if the editor suddenly decides it doesn't work. A case in point was when the *Mirror* revived Cassandra, the acerbic and grumpy anonymous columnist who was the talk of Fleet Street for 30 years in the middle of the last century. Freelance Jonathan Margolis had been a fan of the column since his teens, and got himself into the editor's office to offer himself as the new Cassandra for the new, serious, post–9/11 *Mirror*. What happened next was every freelance's dream: Piers Morgan, the editor, was as keen on the idea as he was. It then turned, as Margolis described in the *Press Gazette* in October 2003, into what sounded like a freelance's nightmare. The column simply didn't make it into the paper sometimes, without explanation; it didn't strike the chord with today's *Mirror* readers that it had 50 years ago, and the whole thing was dropped.

This highlights another problem for freelances: the speed with which things can go out of fashion. What seems a good idea for a column now can seem terribly dated in a year's time, and there are more freelances out there all pitching ideas for what seems like a better column.

Another difficulty for freelances is that their commissioning contact may suddenly move on or even be fired herself. Freelances spend ages building up a rapport with a commissioning editor, but suddenly the person looking after that section changes, and the contact-building has to start all over again. The new person naturally has a number of freelance chums herself, who will be on to their friend within seconds of hearing about the new job.

Some freelances cover news, but this is likely to be successful only if they have built up a solid knowledge of a particular area the paper or magazine wants covered. Freelances sometimes work up quite disparate areas of expertise, and write regularly on one topic for one paper, and on something quite different for another. The secret here is to become an expert in some issue that a paper is unlikely to have a staff person to cover – perhaps alternative energy sources, or road haulage, or acupuncture. Then, obviously, you pray for a massive scandal to emerge about acupuncturists, and hope that the paper will call on your expertise to give weight to their coverage.

Another group of freelances are those who work in an entirely different job and write about that job for a paper or magazine. This could be anything from Jonny Wilkinson writing about place-kicking during the Rugby World Cup, to a local council official having a column about conservation in the local paper. A headteacher might write regularly on issues in education, a doctor about a specialisation in a health magazine, an academic about his subject in a broadsheet newspaper.

The advice to these people is probably, 'don't give up the day job'. This kind of freelancing is very much the icing on the cake, and it can dry up as suddenly as it starts. There can be a bit of tension here: the headteacher, for instance, will be earning a good salary, and may be prepared to accept quite a low fee simply for the fun of seeing his or her name in print. This does not help regular freelances who are trying to make a living from their work.

To those who have never done it, freelancing can seem like a good idea for young parents. It can and does work for some, but the idea that you can change a nappy while dreaming up a 2,000-word feature on public finance initiatives is not always borne out by reality. The same points apply as above: you are more likely to be successful if you are already known as a feature writer and have contacts both on magazines and in the area you are trying to cover. If you need to be organised as a freelance feature writer, you need to be ten times more organised to do it in between the school run and the visits to the orthodontist.

The really lucky writers of **me columns** manage to combine the two: complete the school run, wash the football kit, argue with the nanny, and then moan about it all in print in a weekend paper. However, thankfully in my view, there are not many freelances doing this, and it certainly looks more dependent on luck than anything else. Again, success is more likely for those who have already built up a reputation as a comic writer on other issues – film perhaps, or rock music – who can then move on to nappies and buggies.

Freelance designers

As more and more charities, NHS trusts and the like need their own newsletters, freelance designing is a flourishing growth area. Sometimes these freelances work on their own, sometimes, together with one or two other people, they set up a small company. All this has become much easier with the arrival of the internet and email. Probably the most usual pattern for this is that the client generates the editorial material and pictures, emails everything to the designer, who builds the pages and sends them back for proofreading. Sometimes the freelance writes some of the material as well, from reports and other documents, and possibly commissions some of the pictures, using freelance photographers.

It would be impossible to start up like this without several years' experience as a sub and page designer, with plenty of general skills at problem solving. And embarking on a freelance career is also dependent on having contacts, keeping them alive, and making more. If the freelance is efficient and gets the work done well and to deadline, more commissions usually come by word of mouth. Then such freelances would probably produce their own website and advertise on sites such as charitybuyer.com. Small operations like this obviously depend on being able to keep a number of balls in the air at any one time. It is quite common for a freelancer to be responsible for 15 to 20 different publications, so clear thinking and organisational skills are essential.

  Some people get into this kind of career via a traditional journalistic training, and others via a graphic design qualification. Those with a reporting and news subbing background claim to be able to tell if a publication has been produced by a graphic designer because, they say, it looks more brochure-like and less newsy.

Charlotte Williamson: freelance feature writer

It never occurred to Charlotte Williamson that she would not be a journalist. She knew that was what she wanted to do from a young age. She was drawn to the creativeness of the industry.

After a degree in Japanese at The School of Oriental and African Studies (SOAS) in London, she went on to do a postgraduate diploma in newspaper journalism at City University. She chose the newspaper course as she heard it was the best of the postgraduate courses at City.

Charlotte's first job after finishing her course was as an assistant features writer on the *Evening Standard*. After only one year she was promoted to the position of features writer.

It was not long after this promotion that Charlotte started to feel uncomfortable at the *Evening Standard*. She felt she was no longer able to work at the paper because of its politics. Although the *Evening Standard* had always been part of the *Daily Mail*, this had never caused a problem for Charlotte, until a change of senior management brought a move to the right. When Charlotte felt the time was right to leave the *Evening Standard*, she was fortunate to have a number of contacts on national papers such as *The Observer*, *The Guardian*, *The Daily Telegraph* and *Time Out* magazine. With these contacts Charlotte found she was able to get freelance work. In fact, she was approached and offered work rather than having to chase freelance jobs herself.

Charlotte now writes a variety of freelance articles, covering various subjects from fashion to relationships. She tends to work mainly for *The Sunday Telegraph* and *Elle*, but she doesn't restrict herself. If Charlotte could only ever write one type of feature, she says without a doubt it would be interviews because she finds these the easiest. Charlotte believes that in order to be a freelance writer, it is important to work in a staff job first. This way, you are able to learn how an office works. Also, people get to know you and what sort of writer you are. This is the best way to make contacts that you are able to approach when you are looking for freelance work.

Charlotte has not had any particularly bad experiences in the journalism industry. However, she was warned that getting paid for freelance jobs is a long process. 'You will be constantly assured that there is a cheque in the post.'

Charlotte has no specific plans for the future; she just loves the fact that as a journalist there are so many different paths you can follow. She has had some radio work and enjoyed that, but she is adamant that she does not want to go into television. Like every journalist, Charlotte would love to write a book some day, but she has no idea what it would be about. Most importantly, she has no regrets because she has achieved her goal of becoming a journalist.

Interview by Liz Dye

Training

- *The NCTJ accreditation*
- *What sort of qualifications are needed*
- *Which sort of training course?*

> 'A pleasant and remunerative income can be earned by those would wish to learn how to write for the magazines and newspapers.'
>
> > Advertisement in *The Times* in 1910 for the British School of Journalism, Bloomsbury Square
>
> '(Bateson): "Did you ever take a Correspondence School?" (Boot): "No."
> Bateson looked disappointed. "Oh dear, aren't they a good thing? They're terribly expensive."
> "I expect they are a very good thing."
> "You do think so, don't you? I'm a graduate of the Aircastle School. I paid fifteen shillings a month and I got a specially recommended diploma. That's how I got taken on the *Beast*."'
>
> > Evelyn Waugh, *Scoop*

The training of print journalists is in some disarray. No one knows how many people get into journalism each year, or how they managed it. No one knows how many of them have been taught shorthand, media law, or public affairs. And no one really knows whether many people care, although the one thing that can be said is that the government doesn't care much.

In 2002 the government established the Publishing National Training Organisation (NTO), which was intended to cover training issues for the 250,000 jobs in print publishing: newspapers, magazines and books. Its vision was that the NTOs should become 'sector skills councils', responsible for 400,000 jobs, and inevitably the publishing area was seen as too small.

The Publishing NTO, headed by Joanne Butcher, now chief executive of the National Council for the Training of Journalists, was invited to link up with other groups, possibly in the printing or creative industries. The members, including the Newspaper Publishers' Association, the Newspaper Society and the Periodical Publishers Association were unwilling to continue paying to be members of an organisation they regarded as too broad. So in May 2003 the Publishing NTO dissolved itself and nothing has replaced it.

Meanwhile, the picture of journalism training, never especially clear anyway, is murkier than ever with the launch of so many small magazines and newsletters, and because of the arrival of web journalism. There is no overall regulating body, nor could there ever be one now. For many very small organisations, a regulating body would be a hindrance rather than a help: they would rather simply take someone on, keep them if they are good, sack them if they aren't, and if and when they move on, get someone else. These people may become good journalists, but they will do so through their own efforts, and the fact that they are not clutching a training certificate of any kind will probably be irrelevant.

The waters are further muddied by the fact that so many different journalism courses are springing up, many run by FE colleges and universities, but others set up independently by individuals. Some of these different organisations have also got into the relatively lucrative areas of correspondence courses, evening classes and short course teaching. Again, some of these may be good, but certainly some are not.

The NCTJ accreditation

It seems likely that less than half those starting out in print journalism do so under the auspices of the main training body, the National Council for the Training of Journalists (NCTJ). Originally established more than 50 years ago to organise the vocational training and testing of young journalists on regional and local newspapers, the NCTJ sets a series of exams covering all aspects of reporting, from interviewing to reporting from speeches and documents. It sets out syllabuses for law and public administration exams, and will not award its final certificate to anyone who cannot write shorthand at 100 words per minute. Students can take the preliminary exams during a pre-entry course, but the final exams can be taken and certificate obtained only after a period of work on a newspaper. During this time trainees have to produce a portfolio with details of the kind of work done, to show they have dealt with the differing events a reporter might be expected to cover on a regional paper. About 900 students each year take the preliminary exams, and between 500 and 600 the final NCE, but the pass rate for that is about half or less. It is certainly a rigorous test, and most people would not want to see it made easier, but the low pass rate is cause for concern among trainers. The figure of 400 or so who don't go on to the final NCE is made up of some who go to jobs where the training is organised in-house, or to jobs where there is no training scheme, or of course some who go into other fields of work.

Plenty of people get into journalism and succeed without going through the NCTJ scheme, and it has been criticised for a rather old-fashioned approach. It used to be run by journalists who had mostly been through a long training in the provinces, and they seemed perhaps rather unwilling to visualise a radically different method of training. Anthony Delano, senior research fellow in journalism at the London College of Printing, wrote in *Press Gazette* in March 2002: 'The NCTJ is what journalists get when few of us show any real interest in establishing standards for what most (as my research shows) now consider to be a profession.' This view was echoed by many, but everyone now hopes and believes that the arrival of Joanne Butcher as chief executive will be the beginning of a radical reform of the organisation. She is taking soundings from educators and the industry, and looking at many aspects of the NCTJ's activities. It is very much to be hoped that from 2004 there will be some changes to reflect the more diverse ways people now get into and get on in journalism.

The NCTJ accredits several different kinds of course, from block release, to part-time, to three- or four-year degrees, to postgraduate diplomas. These courses must follow the NCTJ syllabuses, make shorthand compulsory and cover all the prescribed areas of reporting. If they are accredited, then they are of a certain reliable standard, but there are plenty of others, notably at present at the three main higher education establishments in London – City University, the University of Westminster and the London College of Printing – that are not accredited and yet run demonstrably very good courses. One of the difficulties for these universities is the insistence on shorthand. The undergraduate courses particularly may have substantial numbers of foreign students, for whom shorthand would be little or no use. It is to be hoped that some of these issues can be resolved in the near future.

What sort of qualifications do I need?

You can begin training as a journalist at any stage from GCSEs onwards. However, in practice most people entering journalism now have a degree, and those who don't almost certainly have A levels.

For A levels, and for the degree for that matter, study what you think you will enjoy studying most. This is also likely to be the subject you will do best at. Even if at 16 you are considering journalism, many would advise against doing a media studies A level. Clearly, this course can be useful, but many journalism educators and employers are prejudiced against media studies. So do this subject if you enjoy it, but don't do it because you think it might be relevant. It may instead be a slight hindrance.

The same applies to a degree course if you plan to go to university. Three years is a long time so choose the subject that you think you will enjoy most and look forward to working at. Take care, if you choose a media studies degree, that it is a highly-regarded course. There are some good media studies degrees, but choose one carefully: try to get as much advice from as many independent people as possible, and ask to see the job outcomes. Again, some employers and educators are prejudiced against media studies as a degree subject, although this may change. Certainly it seems that the good media studies courses have good job outcomes.

A single or joint honours degree course in journalism will probably be quite good fun, but to get the best fun out of it, the student would need to progress through student journalism and work experience during the vacations, culminating, with any luck, in some paid freelance work towards the end of the course. In this way it will be easier to see the point of the whole thing. Those who don't do much outside journalism will find themselves left a bit behind on the degree course, and at the starting post in the race for jobs.

As student debts increase, fuelled by the banks' willingness to lend ever-larger sums of money, there is a likelihood that more young people will choose a degree course that may lead straight to a job, rather than a non-vocational course with the prospect of paying for further postgraduate training.

What about a gap year?

Have a gap year if you want to, either before going to university, or afterwards, or both. Once you start work it will be far harder to stop and take a year off. I have known some students who worked for a couple of years, took a gap year and did get back into a good job. But I know others who set off for a gap year several years ago and haven't been seen since. One of the good points about a gap year before university is that students often have to do a lot of menial work, and this at least brings home the value of an education which will lead to a more challenging job. Don't expect to get much or any journalism work on your travels, though: you might be lucky, but there are thousands of others with the same idea.

A gap year or two would be fine if you intend to follow it with a pre-entry course.

The difficulty about a gap year after a journalism degree is that it is likely that you will probably need to start all over again on work experience and building contacts. The best way to get a job is to get into casual work or more work experience as soon as the degree has ended, and gradually get shifts and then a contract. If a journalism graduate takes a gap year there will be many thousands more graduates out there wanting work. So if you are determined to travel, well go ahead, because you might not get another chance in the next 30 years. But realise that you will not be in quite such a strong position to get a job when you get back, and you may have to start all over again with work experience and building contacts before landing a job.

Which sort of training course?

There are two main routes into journalism. One is to get a job on a paper or magazine which, in return for your work, will see that you get trained either by sending you on courses, possibly following the NCTJ syllabus, or by arranging in-house training. This is known as **direct entry.** In order to get a job like this, apply directly to the editor of a regional or local newspaper for employment as a trainee. Publications are listed in the *Guardian Media Directory,* Benn's *UK Media Directory* and Willing's *Press Guide,* which are available in libraries. There are official entry requirements of five GCSEs, but in practice most of those going into journalism now have a degree.

Trainees are generally required to sign a training contract, which would probably be for 18 months to two years. During this time the employer will train you in practical journalism, media law, short-hand and public affairs or public administration, which covers the complicated areas of local and central government, health authorities and the like. The NCTJ runs a series of exams covering all these topics and students have to pass them before they can consider themselves as qualified. If you can get taken on in this way, it may well be the cheapest way to get in, since someone else is going to pay for part of your training. On the other hand, the pay may not be good, and you are dependent on the quality or otherwise of the training you are given. Several big groups run their own training schemes, sometimes with an in-house course, such as the one run by Trinity Mirror in Newcastle. Other groups, such as Archant and the Kent Messenger series, send their trainees to the Editorial Training Centre in St Leonards-on-Sea. In both these cases, although trainees follow a similar course to that of the NCTJ, they end up with a different diploma. The Editorial Training Centre is fairly typical. During an intensive 15-week course students are taught shorthand to 100 wpm, media law, government, and plenty of practical reporting. The Trinity Mirror course is similar, and there they also emphasise the business side of newspapers: they want their trainees to have a good understanding of a newspaper's position in the market and its readership.

Both these courses take some students who have not got a training contract and are paying for it themselves. Because the courses are so well focused on what the newspapers want, these students are well-placed to get a job at the end. They are not cheap, however.

Even though these big groups organise training, many of the big regional newspaper groups are now finding they can take young people who have completed a pre-entry course (see below), or have studied journalism at university, so it seems that they do not need, and are therefore not keen, to train someone from scratch. Some media groups, even if they take someone who has done a degree or pre-entry course, still send them on their own training course. Others slot them into their training programme with short courses building up to the NCTJ or group's own diploma.

Regional newspaper groups often want recruits who are local to the area the paper serves. This would mean, if you had gone away from home to university for three years, perhaps coming back to live at home for a while. The papers say they do this because they want to serve their local community, and employ reporters who belong to that community, but it may equally well be to do with the fact that they are not prepared to pay the kind of salary which would enable someone to rent a flat.

Some newspapers use a block release or day release scheme to train their new recruits. They might learn on the job for a while, and then do an intensive eight weeks at an FE (further education) college, or they might go there once a week.

The second route into journalism, which is becoming much more common, is to complete a **pre-entry course**, for which the student will probably have to pay, and then seek work at the end of that. This is obviously more attractive to the employers, because they are then getting a recruit who, depending on the quality of the course followed, may be competent to work as a qualified reporter from day one.

The pre-entry course could be anything from a degree to a nine-month postgraduate diploma, to a short 10- or 12-week course at a college. Many are run at FE colleges, universities and at various independent centres that have sprung up around the country, particularly in the south-east. There are also correspondence and part-time courses, as well as evening classes. Many but not all of these courses are accredited by the NCTJ. Then there are other courses that are 'recognised by the National Union of Journalists' though this should not be regarded as official accreditation.

The cost of all these courses varies wildly, and price may not necessarily be a pointer to quality: some extremely expensive courses are not brilliant, while cheaper ones may be valuable because the college has secured funding from the government or the EU.

The course you choose will depend a great deal on your age when you decide to embark on a career in journalism. If you decide at 17 that this might be your chosen career, then you might consider a degree involving journalism. If you are not afraid of the financial implications, then do a non-vocational degree, but expect to pay for a journalism course of some sort when you graduate. If you decide on journalism at some stage during university, then the sensible thing would be to apply for all the training posts you can find, but you may well have to pay for your own postgraduate course.

Postgraduate options are vast, ranging from MAs, to nine-month diplomas, to shorter 'fast-track' courses. Many are aimed at local or regional newspaper work, but they would be relevant to someone wanting to work in B2B (business-to-business, or trade) magazines as well.

There are also courses specifically for magazine journalism and the best ones are accredited by the Periodicals Training Council (PTC), part of the Periodical Publishers Association. They include the postgraduate diploma at City University, and new courses at Harlow College, Brighton College and Liverpool Community College. These courses seem very reliable, and the PTC takes great care over its accreditation procedure, looking particularly at job outcomes, so a course with the PTC stamp can be relied upon.

There are a few press photography courses, the best known being the NCTJ-accredited course at the Norton Centre at Sheffield College. It is a two-term course of intensive training in press photography and has a very good record on job outcomes. Students vary from those who have just finished degrees, to others who have worked in other areas but have become very keen to be press photographers. The college also has a course on photojournalism, which involves some writing as well. The London College of Printing also runs well-respected courses. There are plenty of degree courses in photography on offer, but if you are interested in press photography, make sure you choose one which seems appropriate.

Imperial College and Birkbeck College, London, as well as Bath University, run courses on science communication. These might be relevant for a science graduate who wants to get into journalism, but they also provide training for those who want to work on specialist peer-reviewed journals.

Many involved in journalism would be surprised to hear that some courses existed nearly 100 years ago, and that at least one became affiliated to London University: the students were addressed by the editor of *The Times*, (see epilogue page 211). The course must have disappeared some time before the current journalism teaching began at Cardiff and City Universities in the 1970s. Correspondence courses are among the longest-standing types of training for journalists: Evelyn Waugh's young character Bateson went on one in the 1930s. He may be right to be worried about it, as it can be difficult to pin down exactly how good a correspondence course is. Do what Bateson did: ask the advice of a senior journalist. But ask several, not just Boot, and ask around before doing the course, not afterwards.

The evening classes available at lots of colleges may be quite fun and a chance to meet like-minded people, but they are not likely to be much use in getting a job. Two hours a week for a term or so might be a useful and interesting introduction, but it is not going to be anything like intensive enough to prepare anyone for paid journalistic work, unless they were very good to start with. If you are serious about journalism, save up for a more substantial course.

Whatever course you are contemplating, the main advice is to try to discover exactly what the job outcomes are. You should ask to see a list of alumni from the course, with details of what they are doing now. Then embark on your first piece of investigative journalism: track down some of those who did the course and ask what they think of it. It is also a good idea to ask advice from any other contacts one may have, or ask around when doing work experience. However if, as is quite likely, the person you talk to says that the only possible way into journalism is the way he or she did it, take that with a pinch of salt. The fact is that almost every journalist over 50 started working without having done a course, but the majority in their 20s have now done a course before they start their jobs. So it is probably better to try to find out how the younger people got where they are, than expect to get into journalism the way we all did in the 1960s and 1970s.

I have lost count of the number of older journalists who have said to me: 'But is it really *possible* to teach *journalism*?' This is because they learned mostly on the job, with perhaps a block release course of a few weeks. Of course it is possible to teach journalism in a classroom, and there are thousands out there in senior editorial positions now who began their journalistic lives in a classroom. However, as with many other professions, good journalists learn new skills and ways of doing their job throughout their career. You have only got to look at a newspaper or magazine from 20 years ago to see how so much has changed, and how necessary it is to keep up to date with fresh ways of doing things if one wants to stay in the job.

Adding to the confusion about courses is the exponential rise in the number of journalism degree courses. In 2003 the Universities and Colleges Admissions Service (UCAS) listed 603 courses (for entry in 2004) with the word journalism in the title, and there are another 3,594 with the word media or media studies in their title. Since a university degree course is unlikely to be viable without at least 30 students, and probably needs more than that, this means rather more than 125,000 graduates coming onto the market each year who may want to work in journalism or related fields. Then there are hundreds more students completing all the various pre-entry courses each year as well. At best, there are likely to be between 20,000 and 30,000 jobs available each year, as people retire or leave the industry. That leaves a lot of disappointed young people.

Of course, this isn't a simple subject and there are very many factors involved, but the universities' need for 'bums on seats' regardless of job opportunities and outcomes has not created a happy situation. Our leaders have done the nation's youth a disservice by allowing this free-for-all to happen. The message for a sixth former who is thinking of a journalism degree course is the same as for all the other courses: do some research, find out the job outcomes of graduates, try to find out how each university is regarded by those in newspapers and magazines. And, sadly, realise that with the kind of competition outlined above, a degree is not going to lead to a job unless you have used part of every vacation to gain work experience, and with any luck towards the end, freelance work.

Entry to courses at FE colleges is by application to the NCTJ, to undergraduate courses through UCAS, and to postgraduate courses by applying to the universities. For courses at the independent training centres you would apply directly to them.

Degree course students may be able to get some funding depending on their circumstances. Some local authorities may help with shorter courses. For postgraduate courses there are a very few bursaries available, and in reality, many people, not just undergraduates, go into debt while completing these courses. There are more details of where to find out about course listings in Chapter 12.

10

Getting a job

> Katherine, it turned out, wanted 'some advice about getting into journalism'. Odd, that. Everyone I know under 25 wants to be a journalist and everyone I know over 25 is a journalist and wants desperately to be something else. Anyway, what's to advise? Get a famous dad, pretend you can type, and don't take the first salary they offer you.
>
> Giles Coren, *The Times*, 22 February 2003

There is, sadly, a lot of truth in Giles Coren's advice. Asked what newspaper she read, someone told me the other day, 'Any paper without a Coren writing in it,' which may considerably limit her choice. Fortunately there are also plenty of ways in for those without famous names.

Far more people get jobs in journalism each week than one would think from the number of job advertisements there are around. Most of the grand newspapers and magazines, the nationals, the big regionals and the glossies hardly ever advertise their job vacancies. Quite a number run training schemes which are never advertised either. This may be partly a point of honour ('We assume there are enough people out there who will ask to come and work here anyway'), and partly to test possible recruits – persistence and determination are both highly valued qualities in journalism.

Most people get in by completing a college-based or employer-based training scheme, and/or by getting into an office to do work experience and proving themselves that way. Then it is often necessary to do casual shifts before being offered a contract. Others get into an office as an assistant or secretary and gradually work their way across to the journalism side. Even if a job is advertised, and there is a conventional interview procedure and then a job offer, the first few months will be very much a trial period.

Getting a journalistic job in the public and charity sectors – writing and producing newsletters and so on – is likely to be through the more conventional route of advert, shortlist, interviews and so on.

So, scan the job ads: the *Press Gazette* and *The Guardian* Media Section on Mondays are the main places to look. Don't waste your time or theirs by applying for jobs for which you are patently unqualified. But do try for those for which you are nearly qualified. You never know, they might not like the other applicants, or they might simply take a shine to you.

Meanwhile, get lots of work experience, and settle down to some serious research, using Willings *Press Guide*, Benn's *Media*, or *The Guardian Media Guide*, and begin the spec letters. These letters might ask for any or all of the following: a job, a trial, a chance to do a few shifts, or, if you haven't got enough, simply work experience.

Making yourself into a journalist

Read lots

To get a job in journalism, or even some work experience, you are going to need to show that you are fascinated by newspapers and magazines. You should read a great variety of them, think critically about them, and have some ideas of your own. You ought to have thought a bit about every national newspaper. Start with one you know. If your family reads the *Daily Mail*, read that carefully for a week. Then get the *Express*, its main rival, every day for a week and compare the two. Which is better, and why? Then branch out – look at *The Times* or *The Telegraph*, how do they compare with the *Mail*, what sort of stories does the *Mail* cover that they don't, and why? The national newspapers, apart from the *Daily Star* and the *Financial Times*, fall roughly into rival pairs: *The Times* and *The Telegraph*, *The Guardian* and *The Independent*, *The Mail* and *The Express*, *The Sun* and *The Mirror*. So think about these pairs: which is the more successful, and why? You don't need to make a labour of it, but it is worth making some notes of your opinions of the various papers, a sort of reading diary. Then repeat the exercise a few months later and see whether your opinions have changed, or maybe the papers themselves have changed.

Do the same thing with the Sunday papers. Buying lots of Sunday papers can be expensive, so see whether friends and neighbours have other papers that you can look at when they have finished with them. If you have a friendly newsagent, you might find that if you go in latish on Sunday they will give you a lot of the magazines and other sections from several Sundays. It seems they need return only the main news section to get the credit for unsold papers, so some newsagents are glad to get rid of the tons of other newsprint. Do the same exercise with magazines. If *Heat* is your Bible then buy a rival magazine, such as *Now*, and compare the two. Is your loyalty misplaced?

Read the *Press Gazette* regularly. Apart from job ads, it has a great deal of extremely useful and interesting news about every aspect of journalism, and will be a great help in understanding how the industry works.

Who are your heroes?

This is a favourite question at college or job interviews, and would-be journalists who can't name a single professional they admire will look a little unfocused, to say the least. In your reading, try to pick out one or two reporters, columnists or feature writers you particularly like. Make a point of reading their work. Look at another paper or magazine and try to find their equivalent on that paper. Is your hero still the best? Why?

Read a book

(Yes, or even several!) Chapter 12 has a list of a few of the most interesting books by journalists, but there are many more. There are collections of published pieces, which can be interesting in seeing how a writer's style has developed, or indeed if it has developed at all or stayed pretty much the same. There are books that are basically extended pieces of journalism, usually about wars or other dramatic events. There are autobiographies, and biographies of other figures.

John Simpson writes about his work as a foreign correspondent. Max Hastings, the former editor of *The Daily Telegraph* and *The Evening Standard*, has written about his reporting career, but has also written about the pleasures of fishing. Bill Bryson, former sub-editor on *The Times* and *The Independent*, specialises in making his travels sound deliberately unglamorous. Reading some of these will give you an insight into some aspects of journalism, give you an understanding of different writing styles, tell you something about recent world events, and last, but not least, give you something to talk about in interviews.

Compare TV, radio and print journalism

Watch the TV news in the evening, and make a quick list of the main stories in the order that they appear. Make a 'newslist' of what one national has the following morning – in order, lead story, second main front page story, main story on page 3, and so on. Compare it with the TV list. They will be different. Why?

Do the same exercise several times, and think about the different news values between TV and a national paper. Do the same with radio. Compare the newslists of the TV and the newspaper with those on the radio. They will be different as well. Why? Which two are the most similar? Why?

Compare pictures

Get two or three rival, or completely different, national papers. Look at their front page pictures, and try to work out why the different editors chose what they did. If one paper went for a completely different picture from everybody else's, why do you think they did that? Does it say something about the type of paper it is, or who they think their readers are?

Repeat exercises like this just before you go to a job or course interview so that you can show you have thought about some of the issues involved in making a paper.

Writing

Write for school/college/university magazines and papers, obviously. There are websites for students and would-be journalists, where you can post articles you have written. Consider making your own website, perhaps about some type of music that interests you, or some other hobby. It isn't all that difficult, and you can then play around with design, put up pictures that interest you, and so on. Beware of internet stalkers of course, and put up no more than an ordinary mugshot of yourself. Or perhaps create a website about your school or college sports team, or forthcoming club night, play or charity effort.

If you are doing some interesting travelling keep a journal. You are highly unlikely to get it published (sorry, but there are **many**, many, thousands of students out there who would like to see their death-less travel prose in print). But it will be helpful to you in your writing to compare your own journal with what does get into print. When you get back, search on the internet for articles about wherever you went, and compare them. If you are emailing home, don't just crash out an email, but spend some time thinking about it and making notes before you go to the internet café. Then when you are there, try to turn your email home into a well-shaped piece of writing.

Your travel journal will be of great interest to you and your grandchildren in 40 years' time. And when you become rich and famous, maybe you can get it into print then. You wouldn't be the first: Patrick Leigh Fermor published his gap-year walk across Europe (though it wasn't called gap year then) 47 years later, when he had become a highly acclaimed author. Think about other outlets for your writing, such as local community newsletters. Write a well-crafted letter to your granny or someone abroad. And keep up with any other writing – song lyrics, raps, poetry. Or start work on the great 21st-century novel.

Learn grammar and spelling

If you are thinking 'I don't need to do that because the Word program does it all for me', then think again. Spelling and grammar checks do help with a few things sometimes, but in general they really only provide a test to make sure you get right what you already know. Some word processing software is programmed with American spelling, so you need to be able to spell yourself to work out whether your computer can spell in British English. Also, computers generally struggle with homonyms – they often can't work out which of two possible spellings is the right one for the context. The most obvious example is the different uses of there and their. And the grammar suggestions are often idiosyncratic, to say the least.

But the real disaster is when you run the spellcheck at speed just before submitting the copy. The reporter goes into autopilot, clicking on yes to all the Word suggestions, and it is then that proper names go wrong. It was thanks to spellchecking that *The Times* recently had a story about a hitherto unknown judge, Herald Garden, instead of Gerald Gordon. The best one I have seen is the author of *Midnight's Children* who turned up in a student's story as Salmon Residue.

The spellcheck is just about useable if the writer knows she can't spell and uses it as a dictionary, stopping and checking words as she goes along. Then there is no danger of clicking through quickly with the spellcheck when the story is complete and making things worse rather than better.

The majority of schools stopped teaching grammar and spelling seriously in the 1970s. I still can't see why. When I look back at the chemistry I was taught, I cannot think of a single time when that knowledge has been of any use to me at all. But knowing what the passive tense is, and that lively and lovely are adjectives rather than adverbs, has been of regular use all my life. And sadly, in spite of much talk and hand-wringing for the past 20 years or so, grammar and spelling do not seem to have been taken up again. One of the reasons for this may be that many of the teachers are the children of the 1970s and they haven't been taught this kind of thing themselves. It seems unlikely that there will be a radical improvement in the average school leaver's standard of English in the near future. I've seen postgraduates with Oxford Firsts who haven't grasped the apostrophe rules, so one assumes that all along the line their tutors either didn't know them either or didn't care.

Anyone who is serious about any sort of career involving writing needs to do some work themselves. There are some book suggestions in Chapter 12, and some of them are even quite fun to read. There are websites giving advice on grammar. If you know that you have difficulties with grammar and spelling set yourself some tasks. There are only about ten basic errors that people make and if you can learn not to make those, you will save yourself, your tutors and your future news editors much grief. Write out the rules in your own words. Make flash cards. Read a grammar book at the bus stop. This doesn't make you a saddo, it just makes you someone who doesn't want to be hampered by an easily surmountable problem. Read lots, including newspapers, and especially tabloids such as the *Sun*, and national news magazines in which there are almost never any errors.

Learn computer skills

Every year first jobbers are more computer literate than their predecessors were the previous year. This is the case for every kind of job, whether in teaching, medicine, law or journalism. Barristers and consultants may not like to acknowledge this, but surely in 10 or 15 years' time barristers will type their own opinions straight into a computer and consultants will deal with their own notes. It will simply be quicker and easier than dictating to a secretary.

Good computer skills are essential for almost every job, so the sooner you learn them the better. To make yourself employable, you should at the least be able to touch type reasonably quickly (say 35 words per minute), have basic word processing skills such as moving paragraphs and making headings and boxes, be able to use spreadsheets and turn them into pie or bar charts, and search the internet quickly and efficiently.

If you are planning to do a training course or degree, you would do well to acquire all the above before you start it. And check that the course you are planning to do will train you well in desktop publishing skills with software such as Photoshop and QuarkXPress or Adobe InDesign. Although lots of would-be journalists can see themselves only as news or feature writers, there is no doubt that plenty of people get jobs on magazines, and sometimes newspapers, on the strength of their desktop publishing. Some major papers are replacing Quark with InDesign, which is possibly cheaper. But this, and the fact that some big organisations have their own tailor-made systems, doesn't matter all that much. If you can use Quark, and are generally handy with a computer, you will be able to transfer to a similar system fairly easily. Of course almost everyone plans to be a picture-bylined Writer (with a capital W) but almost certainly, unless you are the next Julie Burchill, you need to get the first job first. I recently came across a student journalist who could write beautifully. The features tutors loved him. But it took him ages to get his first job because all he could do was write. If he had got really stuck in with QuarkXPress, and also improved his ability to research and write short, accurate, news stories, he would have found it much easier to get his first job. He is now a bylined Writer, but it took him longer to get there than it should have done.

Think like a journalist

In every group of students, there will be one or two to whom all the others tell their troubles. They always make extremely good journalists. You need to become the kind of person that other people tell things to, and one way to do this is to get into the habit of talking to people, and listening to them. I have uncovered half a dozen good local stories simply by talking to the check-out operators in the supermarket. And their tales about the doings of the Friday night singles shoppers, though in some cases not publishable, certainly make good dinner party stories.

I had a conversation with a young Oxford graduate once about whether or not he talked to his hairdresser. No, he didn't. 'There isn't anything I could talk to her about' he said. 'We have nothing in common at all.' Well I don't have a huge amount in common with mine. He is a gay New Zealander whose partner is HIV positive, and they are active in the London club scene. His life could hardly be more different from that of a middle-aged college lecturer with a family and a nice garden. But we manage to chat together for a couple of hours every few weeks. He is interested in people, and so am I.

If all the above sounds daunting, and/or too much trouble, take heart. It is worth acquiring many of the traits outlined above anyway: some of them will be of great use in all sorts of jobs, including, obviously, hairdressing.

Work experience

It is only 15 or so years ago that the home editor of *The Independent*, when it was at its most successful and famous, was astonished to receive a letter from a young woman with a good degree, and a year or two in good non-journalistic jobs, writing that she would like to come to work at the paper FOR NOTHING. How things have changed. As its reporting staff has shrunk, *The Independent* in recent years has occasionally been almost overrun with students on work experience.

Many other careers have always had a work experience system, but it may have gone under another name. Student teachers have always done many months of (unpaid) teaching practice. Medical students spend a couple of years on wards, watching what the doctors do, before they qualify. This system has been extended into many more spheres. Big law, accountancy, property and other firms all offer structured work placement schemes, without which it would be harder to get a training contract. It seems the structured work placement has replaced the 'milk round' – the system where firms toured universities holding career seminars and conducting preliminary interviews. Now they expect the would-be employees to come to them during the vacation and show what they can do.

This is particularly true of journalism, where work experience is now the key to the job. There are still a few people who get good jobs without ever having set foot in a newspaper office – as most of us did 20 or 30 years ago. But having helped several hundred students get jobs over the past few years, and talked to many more young journalists, I believe that very few people get a first job in journalism without around four to five months of unpaid work experience.

Take heart: in the film industry the norm can be more like a year, and there the first paid job may also be at a lower salary than for many first jobs in journalism. It is essential to try for work experience in lots of different places, for many reasons. Many of the places you try will turn you down. At the last minute a paper you were relying on will have a change of news editor, and the new person will ban work experience the day before you were due to start. Also, it is possible for even the most charming person to have a really nasty time on a work placement. They didn't know you were coming, there is nowhere to sit, nobody will give you any work to do, and when you ask to go out with a senior reporter your request is greeted with a sigh. When they hear at the end of the first week that you are expecting to stay for another week there is an even bigger sigh, and so on. This is why it is essential to get several different placements. If one is the placement from hell, the next will be better fun.

Work experience is effectively training. On a good placement a student could expect to learn from senior practitioners, get some practice in and some feedback on work, receive some useful advice, and end up with some cuttings for the portfolio. Yet another point about work experience is that it proves to a potential employer that you know what the job is like, and therefore your decision to pursue it is a valid one.

Obtaining work experience, especially during holiday periods, is getting harder all the time. Some of the most popular papers and magazines now interview people for work experience, and expect them to arrive with a portfolio of cuttings before they will consider allowing them to work for nothing. For students, work on student papers is a start, or there are student websites for which you can write material. Anything which will make your CV stand out from someone else's will help.

Applying for work experience is exactly the same as applying for a job. You need a well-polished CV and a decent covering letter. News editors get plenty of CVs which would qualify for work experience, so the letter must say something else about you which will make you stand out. 'I know Peebles very well, having lived here all my life....' 'For several years I have followed every development in the world of hiphop/performance cars/rabbits/containerisation.' You can expand on some point in the CV 'I have designed all the pages for the *Warwick Boar* for the past six months...' and so on.

Ring your target publications and find out the name of the right person to write to. (It might be editor, news editor, or editor's secretary.) Journalism is about finding things out, and a would-be journalist who can't even find this out will not go far. Whoever it is, **get the name and title right**. A letter which starts Dear Sir/Madam deserves to be binned and probably will be. Some publications make a point of saying they do not offer work experience, because they will take only those who are persistent enough to get a name and write in anyway.

There may well be no answer to the letter. So after about ten days, ring, ask politely to speak to the right person, and ask what are the chances. Make sure you have in front of you the name of the person you want to speak to. Practise a few scenarios.

If they say they are booked up for a year, ask to be put on the list for next year; if they say they don't offer work experience, ask them to reconsider 'because I have set my heart on a job with *Cage and Aviary Birds*'. Be charming and polite throughout, but persistent. It may genuinely be that they don't offer placements because there simply isn't enough for someone to do. You will have to assess this. But remember that persistence counts for a lot, and remember, too, that charm and politeness count for nearly as much.

For the first attempt at work experience in a professional office, aim for a small publication with a small staff. If you have no work experience on your CV, don't even waste a stamp writing to *The Guardian* or *Vogue*. By all means take it up if you know someone who might get you into a national newspaper or magazine for a couple of weeks, but be prepared to have a frustrating and generally rather unpleasant time, watching other people doing things, and with no one having the time to talk to you or explain what is going on. You will probably have a far better time on a small local paper or small magazine, where people will have time to help you and give you a chance to see what you can do.

One new graduate (now a foreign correspondent for a national) went for three weeks to the *Ballymena Guardian*, a tiny paper with a staff of about seven journalists. He had a brilliant time, ended up writing masses of stories and came back with pages of cuttings. Once you have one placement on your CV, and with any luck some cuttings and a reference, you can approach a bigger paper or magazine.

At first, it will take 10 or 20 letters to yield one placement. But don't give up. The more experience you get on your CV, and the more cuttings in your portfolio, the easier it gets. Visit a newsagent near where you live. You will probably be amazed to find there are several local papers on display, when you thought there was only one. Try all of them. Think laterally as well: where in the country do you have a friend/auntie/granny who could put you up while you do some work experience?

When you have spent some time, or at least booked some time, on a small paper, think about a magazine. If you live in the country, there are many 'county' magazines. If you live near a biggish city such as Bristol or Birmingham there will be magazine publishing companies there. There are hundreds in London.

The specialist magazines are not such a good idea, unless you are something of an enthusiast yourself. The dozens of gardening magazines, for example, will be looking only for people with some knowledge. The same goes for cookery and the big customer magazines linked to supermarkets, such as *Waitrose Food Monthly*. Some of these are brilliant magazines, but realistically they offer few opportunities for a non-expert to do much. If, however, you are genuinely keen on cars, or computer games, specialist magazines covering these areas would be a good idea.

On the whole, unless you already have a lot of work experience, you are likely to have far less rewarding work experience on the well-known high-profile magazines such as *Vogue, Cosmopolitan* or *Heat*, supposing you can even get into them. Some of the big glossies have a very well organised system which employs a rolling scheme of work placement people. The most recent recruit is shown the ropes by the outgoing person so that the magazine gets some useful running around done and they don't need to tie up one of the staff to explain the job. On the big fashion glossies the work of organising the clothes called in for fashion shoots might occupy two work experience people for most of the time. At least there is no danger of being bored because there is not enough to do. The fashion editor might decide: 'What we want is spangly jumpers', and an assistant will then ring round all the fashion houses. Dozens of spangly jumpers arrive by courier. They all have to be unpacked, logged, and hung up. Sooner or later, whether they are actually photographed or not, they have all got to be packed up and sent back. Plenty of stuff goes missing, adding to the general stress of the whole thing. It is hard work, you might get expenses, you won't get a Prada bag (though the fashion editor probably will), and you probably won't get a job. The work experience person is effectively an editorial assistant for two months, and if they have six people like this coming in every year, only one of them (if that), is likely to get a contract. In general, the glossier the magazine, the glossier the Sloane Ranger who actually gets the job. Sadly, it probably won't be the journalism degree, the shorthand, the knowledge of media law, or the cuttings; it will be the accent. Some of the big magazines are the worst offenders in the work experience racket, but while there are young women out there with money to live on and time on their hands, it is unlikely things will change much. Much the same sort of thing happens on the upmarket decorating magazines, where the interior design editor will decide that what we need this month is material/china/ candlesticks/glasses decorated with butterflies. The only difference here is that much of it is breakable, so there is even more work to do unpacking and packing the stuff up.

You may not have very good work experience on the major news magazines such as *The Spectator* and the *New Statesman*. Freelances contribute most of the material, so the opportunity for actual writing may be limited. But the smaller political magazines, such as *Red Pepper,* may be a good place to try.

One of the very many B2B magazines may provide a better experience. Many have plenty of short news items about developments in the world of nursing/property/media/design/law, etc., which gives a trainee a good chance to get a couple of cuttings.

Many young people will have set their hearts on music magazines, and while there are plenty out there, there are also a great many people who want to work for them. So wait until you have got some experience before trying them. The same applies to sports magazines.

The Face, now defunct, used to ask work experience applicants to send a list of ideas they would like to see in the magazine. One wag sent in a drawing of a face, and did get the placement, for being witty. But that joke will work only once. In another case a young woman sent the news editor a letter on rainbow-striped paper, saying, 'I was told I needed to catch your eye so I hope this letter does.' She got the placement and is now a senior journalist on a (different) national.

For those of us who have been around in journalism for quite a while, the whole work experience system seems slightly like a return to a Victorian model of apprenticeship. In those days a family paid a craftsman to train their son or daughter, and the apprentice signed an agreement about hard work and good behaviour. After a period, possibly of some years, of earning little or nothing, the young person was qualified to start paid work themselves. We have got back to that, with parents helping their offspring with free accommodation and/or pocket money, or with the young person financing work experience by doing bar work to pay the rent. The National Union of Journalists has very firm views about what it calls 'the work experience racket': 'There is rampant exploitation of student journalists and recent graduates by publications abusing 'work experience',' says the union. It is right in some cases, and it is not alone in feeling strongly about this. However this is the way things are in many different careers, so it seems unlikely to change in the near future. What is important is to make sure that the work experience is a learning experience. A good news editor ought to be sure to give some help to every work experience person, whether it is spending time explaining how their story could have been better, ensuring that they are taken on jobs with seniors, or simply making sure that some of their questions get answered. Then it is fair to expect some work from them in return.

Having a good time on work placements

Some work experience is brilliant, and some is horrid. Sometimes a student goes to a paper and has a great time, and the following year another goes to the same place and has a miserable time. Sometimes it is to do with the news editor. Sometimes, often perhaps, it is to do with the student. A positive attitude and a determination to get something useful out of the experience, will certainly make it more likely that it goes well. Being one of those people for whom the glass is half full rather than half empty is probably a good lesson for life. But it is an essential lesson for work experience. If you begin it with a simmering resentment about being exploited, it might be better to consider another career directly. Those who are thinking positively and smiling from the start will have the best time.

Before

1. Read several issues of the paper/magazine thoroughly so you know the style and what stories they cover. Research on the internet beforehand to see if any major issues have come up, either in that geographical area if it is a newspaper, or subject area if it is a magazine. If the publication has rivals, look at those too.
2. Check out the city or town beforehand. If you don't live there, arrive a day early to get orientated: find out where the major landmarks are.

3. Buy an A–Z map. When you are asked to go somewhere try not to make the first question 'How do I get there?'

Be prepared

1. Get there early, dressed appropriately. A newspaper will probably expect you to be wearing a suit or at least (for men) a tie and jacket – certainly not jeans. If it is *Kerrang!* or *Straight No Chaser* you would clearly be out of place in a suit.

2. Make sure you take the letter confirming the placement, with the name of the person with whom you organised it. Have a note, from your research and reading, of the editor's and any other senior names. Don't be surprised if they have forgotten that you were coming. You can produce the offer letter, so you will be able to say 'I fixed this up with XX in January.'

3. Arrive with a new notebook of your own – it's better than having to ask for one. Also, you can have made notes in it of the senior people's names, and one or two other important things, such as the office phone number. Then, if you go out, you can ring in easily. Date the notebook, write your name in it, and write down EVERYTHING anyone tells you, whether it is the name of the person at whose desk you are sitting (so you can charm them when they get back) or directions to the nearest pub. It is fine to ask anything once, but make sure you don't have to ask twice.

Be happy

1. Get the name of everyone else in the office right on day one. (Make secret notes to remind yourself if necessary.) This is not a difficult exercise, unless the office is very large. But it will impress people, and go a long way towards getting people on your side. Remember that on the whole, many journalists regard work experience people as a nuisance. It is naff, when someone asks what you are up to, if you reply 'That bald guy over there suggested I look through these press releases', rather than 'Jim, the news editor, suggested....' This skill of getting people's names right quickly is extremely valuable for journalism, and indeed many other jobs.

2. If they ask you to shadow someone else, when you think you could do a story on your own, don't complain, and simply go along with it for a while. But make sure you write your own version of whatever story you cover, and ask someone to look at it. And keep smiling.

3. If they give you a pile of old press releases, go through them and do your best to find something new. And keep smiling.

4. Get the sandwiches at lunchtime – someone has to. And keep smiling.

5. When you are given a task, write it down in your notebook and make sure you understand exactly what is required AT THE TIME. No one will mind explaining something, especially if you are charming. But they will be irritated if you sit at your desk for half an hour and then go back and say you didn't understand.

6. But asking after half an hour, if you have to, is better than not asking at all and getting it wrong.

7. If, sadly, you do get something wrong, own up immediately. It will almost certainly come out, and you will cause less trouble if you get your hand up as soon as possible.

8. If after three days you haven't done much, ask to go on a story with a senior reporter. Then a day after that, come up with an idea of your own. Think up a feature, or a local angle on a national story. Make sure the story is feasible – so not 'How about I go out and look for a 12-year-old drug trafficker?' Present it briefly and well. If it is a really good story, be prepared for them to take it away from you and give it to a senior reporter (sob).

Don't

1. *Argue.* Sorry, but if your work gets spiked, they are not going to change their minds about the story if you argue, but they'll change their minds about you. It is reasonable to ask politely if someone has time to explain to you what was wrong with it.

2. *Leave shirty notes or send shirty emails.* As a tutor, some of the emails I have had from students beggar belief. Much has been written about how people are far ruder in emails than they would be either face to face or in a letter or phone call. As we all know from various famous cases, emails can be stored, sent on to the editor, passed all round the office and so on. It is one thing for a star columnist to send a shirty email to a newsdesk or chief sub, although several who have done so must have regretted it when it appeared in *Private Eye*. But wait until you are a star columnist before sending one. Every news editor has

a good story about a rude email from a junior, so don't let yours add to the list. For the same reason, obviously, don't send saucy messages to your boyfriend or indeed anyone else.

3. *Gossip.* Journalists are terrible gossips and it is hard to avoid hearing some gossip. But journalists also have a great loyalty to each other, and will take extremely unkindly to a work placement person offering opinions on colleagues and, say, their drinking habits. Also remember that journalism is a very small world indeed. If you start slagging off the news editor at the paper where you did work experience last year, you may find you are talking to that person's partner.

4. *Grab the news editor's phone.* It is hard to believe, but a student on work experience did just that. The placement did not lead to a job.

5. *Fiddle expenses.* Even harder to believe, but another student on work experience tried to do this. Fiddling expenses is the mark of a senior journalist. News desk secretaries are shrewd hawk-like people, and a work experience person is most unlikely to be able to put one over them. Again, no job there.

6. *Ring your boyfriend in New York.* The work experience person who did this at *The Independent* was asked to leave the same day, a great pity as she had just come from New York to do the placement. One good reason not to do this is that calls can now be traced to particular extensions. Another is that you will annoy everyone else in the office beyond belief.

7. *Do other freelance work from the office.* Again, hard to believe, but true, and again, no job there.

Be charming, but persistent

1. Make sure that at the end of your time there they think how happy they would be for you to stay, rather than how pleased they are that you are going.

2. If you are not been given enough to do, find someone who looks busy and ask if you can do any research or run any errands for them.

3. Get the coffee/sandwiches (again).

The smaller the office, the more important the charm point is. In a big regional or national newspaper office the news editor might be quite happy to have someone with a good eye for a story and/or good contacts, but who is a bit of a pain in the neck. Every hack who has worked in a big organisation has met plenty of these people, whose irritating ways are diluted when they are part of a big team. But many first jobs are in very small offices, perhaps of three or four people. They are certain to have a large field of candidates to choose from, and they will choose the charmer every time over someone who seems likely to put their backs up. So spend a lot of time thinking about what kind of impression you are making. Try to put yourself in the position of the middle-aged news editor who has had a satisfying, but not meteoric, career in small magazines, and doesn't want to hear too much about your gap year or student newspaper exploits and ambitions. I listened once as a Reuter trainee explained to an older hack some points about the press in India, where she had spent a few months on a gap year. I had to intervene to tell her that she was talking to a former Delhi bureau chief.

Whether the placement was good or bad, if you have done your best by them, tried to be useful, and been charming as well, you are entitled to a bit of their time. A couple of days before the placement ends make sure that you ask for five minutes with the news editor or features editor you were reporting to. Ask for feedback on your work. Ask to come back for another placement. Ask how you would go about getting a job on the publication. ('Have I got enough work experience yet? Would you recommend the City course?') Ask for any other advice they can give. Ask them to write a reference for you, to go into your cuttings file as proof that you did the work experience. If you did very well, ask for a job. Keep the name and number of the news editor and anyone else who was particularly helpful in your contacts book. And thank the news editor, and everyone you have worked with, for having you. Email or write the following week to thank properly. Contact them again a few months later to remind them who you are, tell them you have started your course, ask for another placement, or whatever.

It is impossible to overestimate the value of charm, willingness and friendliness. Placement people who have plenty of these qualities are far more likely to have a productive time, be asked back, and get a job in the end.

11

CVs and job applications

- *The CV*
- *The covering letter and cuttings*

The CV

In many employment areas the CV (curriculum vitae) is getting longer and longer. This may be partly to do with the growth in what are often called, irritatingly, Human Resources departments (implying that humans are just another resource, like computer hardware, desks and buildings, as if the firm or organisation is anything without them). In HR departments large teams pore over job specifications, promotions policy, employment law and like to give the impression that all employees or would-be employees are about to sue over not being appointed, not being promoted, or not being given two sofas in their office. There is some truth in this of course.

HR people spend a great deal of time crafting lengthy job specifications. A specification for a first job in a charity or local council can run to four or five pages. And it follows that to make sure the CV for that job covers everything, it too will need to be several pages long.

There are model CVs in Microsoft Word, and on many internet sites offering advice. Beware of the internet sites. Many are based in the US, where wordiness is an art form and, in any case, they want you to pay them to write your CV for you. No editor is going to be remotely impressed by a would-be journalist who has not written their own CV.

'Résumé' is an Americanism, and if you use that expression it will give away the fact that you have used a US model to compile your CV. The Word templates look smart, but don't bother to put a paragraph on 'objective' – it should be pretty obvious that your objective is to get a job.

Most journalism (not all, unfortunately) is dedicated to saying things as concisely as possible. Your CV is the first example to your possible future employer of your ability to do this. A news editor simply will not read a lengthy CV. All the stuff some people write at the beginning: 'A friendly and outgoing French graduate who has experience of a number of software applications. . .' will hinder attempts to get into journalism. Chatty material in each section: 'I much enjoyed my stint on the checkout in Sainsbury's where I honed my skills at dealing with people and learnt a great deal about different vegetables...' should be cut to the barest bullet points, or removed altogether.

A CV for an application for a first or second job should be one page if possible, or two if you have done a great deal of work experience. It should be updated regularly to include anything new which might help, and should be angled to show, where possible, that everything you have done is relevant to the job. Temping in telesales provides useful experience in telephone interviewing and is worth mentioning. A junior job in an employment agency might show an ability to keep accurate records and deal with the public. Or a similar job in some council departments might have developed research skills. But keep to pithy single-phrase bullet points. And cut out all the detail about the six bar jobs – unless you are applying for another one, of course.

The growing trend is to put education and jobs/work experience in reverse chronological order, and certainly if you have got something recent and impressive to offer, this would probably be best. Be ruthless about throwing material out as more useful information becomes available. One would expect details of school magazine work on an 18-year-old's CV, but a 20-year-old ought to have something better. Everyone did the school magazine or something similar, but if you have something really impressive – you played cricket for your county under-16 team, or won an award for a website you created when you were 12, then leave that in for a few more years.

Spend plenty of time trying out different designs for the CV, experimenting with columns, different typefaces and settings, maybe even some colour. The trend now is to make the heading your own name, and, obviously, put your phone numbers and email at the top. Many students like to have crazy email addresses, such as funkyprince@hotmail.com or givemethemonkey@hotmail.com. This might be fine for applying to *Loaded*, but consider creating a more sober one if you are applying to the *Financial Times*.

Include all your computer skills (if you haven't got any, acquire some quickly), languages, driving licence and so on, probably under a separate heading of skills. Add a section about interests, but try to make it clear that you are slightly different from the next person. 'Interests: reading and going out' looks so obvious it is naff, but 'reading, especially underground literature from Turkey' or 'music: folktronica and funk' might catch the eye. Of course, don't put down anything which isn't true – it might turn out that the news editor's partner has been translating Turkish poetry for 20 years. And be ready to explain precisely what folktronica is, and why you like it.

Some would-be journalists make a CV which looks like the front of a paper, with a lead story 'Chris Bloggs applies for trainee post' and sidebars about their education and experience. This might be help your CV to stand out from all the others which arrive on the same desk every morning.

An example of a CV follows. It has been deliberately left fairly plain and even average-looking, because it is important for everyone to design their own. Journalism is about producing something different from the next person, and if a news editor is faced one morning with three CVs which have clearly all been designed using the same software package, they will all probably go into the bin.

In theory, a CV should be altered slightly for every job application, to add a phrase highlighting a skill or area of knowledge relevant to this particular job. But the reality is, as we know, that would-be journalists are going to have to make multiple applications, many of them 'on spec' – that is, not in response to an advertisement – simply to get the CV into the news editor's filing system. For this exercise, the CV is probably going to look the same for several applications.

When you think the CV looks perfect, ask someone you know has an eagle eye for errors to check it very carefully. And save it for a couple of days without looking at it, then read it through again very carefully yourself. Errors are spotted far more easily after a day or two of not looking at something. Contrary to popular belief, most journalism is extremely accurate in terms of grammar and spelling, and a news editor will not look favourably on applicants who can't prove they are capable of a high level of accuracy.

Jane Smith

10 The Street
Totsham
Wessex
TH1 4SJ

Date of birth *15.08.81*
janey_smith1891@yahoo.co.uk
07730 607561

PAID JOURNALISM

December 2003 –
Regular evening uploading shifts, *Guardian Unlimited*, inputting material from the newspaper onto the website.

WORK EXPERIENCE

August 2003
Two weeks' work experience at *Totsham Guardian*, paid-for weekly. Covered many small news items, including golden weddings, post office closure, church belfry appeal. Many cuttings. Invited back for two weeks August 2004.

June 2000
One week work shadowing at *Totsham Guardian*.

September 2003
Music Editor of *Cub*, Queen Mary student newspaper, writing and editing material for the music pages, commissioning features, organising coverage of gigs and clubs.

CITY UNIVERSITY AND QUEEN MARY, UNIVERSITY OF LONDON

2002–
Now in second year of joint BA in Journalism and Contemporary History. Extensive work on news and feature writing, interviewing and research. Website building, page design using QuarkXPress and radio work using CoolEdit.

TOTSHAM COMMUNITY SCHOOL

2002: A Levels: History (A), French, English Literature (both B)
2000: 10 GCSEs (6 at Grade A) including Maths, Science double award and English.
Editor, school magazine, 2001.
Managing director of Young Enterprise scheme June 2001, producing postcards from old prints of Totsham, won first prize for best scheme in regional finals. Produced website about the project.

PAID WORK

June 2000–September 2002: Saturday and holiday work at Pizza Parlour, Totsham, waitressing then regular shifts as supervisor, organising staff and dealing with customers.

SKILLS

Fully proficient in Word (35 wpm) Excel, PowerPoint, Access, internet research, QuarkXPress, Photoshop. Website-building using HTML and Dreamweaver.
Learning Teeline shorthand (currently 60 wpm).
French (good), German (basic).

OTHER INTERESTS

Travel (Europe widely, including backpacking extensively in Turkey). Music, especially garage. Currently producing website providing listings of gigs in East London.

REFERENCES – SEE OVER

The covering letter and cuttings

It is likely that a news editor will receive many CVs as good as yours. The covering letter and a sheet of cuttings are important to make your application stand out from the crowd. Contrary to the advice given on some CV software and jobs websites, I believe, after talking to lots of news and managing editors, that the covering letter should be seven or eight short (one or two sentence) paragraphs. This is important to show that you can construct sentences accurately and make them flow well.

The letter should say when you are available for work or work placement, and why you want the job or placement. You need to highlight whatever knowledge you have which might help your case, such as the fact that you have lived in the area all your life, or that *The Guardian* is the only paper you ever want to work for (join the queue). Highlight the skills you have, the other experience you have had, or anything else that might help. If it is for work experience, say you will ring in a couple of weeks to see whether they can fit you in. Above all, the letter must sound enthusiastic. As with the CV, take great care over the final edit, and get someone you trust to check it for you.

With it you should send a sheet of photocopies of some cuttings, if you have some. *Do not under any circumstances send originals.* They are sure to get lost, and if you then ring up asking people to trace them, they will get extremely irritated and make a mental note never EVER to let you into the office. One A4 or A3 sheet with four or five cuttings is probably about right. The news editor is not going to look at them very carefully, but might spare them a glance. Make sure they have reproduced well, and that it is clear what publication they are from, and the date (e.g. *Hullfire*, student newspaper, March 2003). Put your own name at the top in case they get separated from your CV and letter. If you haven't any cuttings, try to think of something else to send. It might be an article from your school magazine, a piece you have managed to get on to a student website, or even a piece you have written for a school assignment. If all else fails, interview an interesting friend or acquaintance and write that up. Anything which shows you have made an effort will help.

Keep a record of where you have applied and when, so that you can judge when to make follow-up phone calls.

The job interview

You have done lots of placements, got lots of cuttings, sent off lots of letters, and finally, you have a job interview. Unfortunately, even at this stage, things are still quite random. Sometimes news editors and others see people when they haven't really got a job to offer, sometimes they think they have got a job to offer, and there has been a change of heart by the managing editor or publisher, and it turns out they haven't. Sometimes it is a preliminary chat, and a candidate might be asked back to see someone else, or do some trial shifts, before a job is offered. The record I have heard of so far is five interviews, all at different times for an (admittedly fairly senior) job on a national paper.

Assuming there is a job on offer, no one wastes time interviewing someone who is not going to be able to do it. If you have got this far, you are qualified for it. Therefore it follows that if you don't get the job, you failed the interview. It sounds a bit brutal put like that, and of course you can and should console yourself with the fact that there may have been someone else with more relevant experience than you have. But it is worth facing up to the fact that whether or not you get the job depends very largely on what might be a relatively brief interview. This is why you should welcome the chance to do tests, trial shifts, or anything else where you can show what you can do.

You should do a huge amount of work beforehand for every interview. And make sure you keep notes of all your research and preparation, as it may well be useful for another interview or trial shift later on.

Funny interview stories abound, many of them apocryphal. There is the one about the hearty (all-male) Oxford college, where sport was considered more important than study. The moment they opened the door, interview candidates were passed a rugger ball by one of the panel. The ones who caught it were offered a place. Those who caught it and passed it straight on to another don across the room were offered an exhibition, and those who did a drop goal into a wastepaper basket gained a scholarship. Preparing for that interview, obviously, involved practising kicking.

But plenty of the anecdotes are true. There have been stories of interview questions getting dafter: 'If you were a fish what sort of fish would you be?' Perhaps this was for someone applying for a post as a stand-up comic. For interviews at one Cambridge college candidates are placed on a chair much lower than the ones the panel sit in, and the panel members sit in the corners of the room so that candidates find themselves swivelling uncomfortably to try to see who is asking which question. The dons had clearly read some manual for a City trading firm, where it was important to see how the candidate coped with stress. But what has stress got to do with successfully studying history at university?

There is a famous postgraduate journalism course where the group being interviewed are given a test, then they are gathered in one room, told they are all rubbish, none will make it as a journalist, and they might as well go home. Then the lecturer departs, leaving his door open. The students who have the courage to follow him and say that they are *not* rubbish earn a place on the course.

It is widely acknowledged that deliberately subjecting the candidate to stress is an important part of the selection process. So you need to be aware that this might happen, and be ready to cope with it.

Preparing for the interview

There are several different areas you need to think about, and be prepared to talk about. They fall into two groups: first, the publication, its style, market, readership, and mission; and second, yourself, how you are going to project yourself, show what you are like and what you can do. You need to think about likely questions, and prepare your answers in both these major areas. Then you also need to prepare some questions to ask the interviewer.

The publication

Know it well. This true story is still hard to believe: a former student got to the final round of interviews for a traineeship at Express Newspapers, publishers of the *Daily Express* and the *Sunday Express*. The interview was on a Monday.

Editor:	'What did you think of yesterday's paper?'
Applicant:	'I didn't read it.'

You couldn't make it up. The editor should have ended the interview there and then, as they were clearly wasting each other's time.

Research the publication's circulation, readership, where it stands in the market, what its rivals are, how long it has been operating, and so on. Scrutinise the local area if it is a regional paper or the latest issues if it is a B2B magazine. This will mean that any questions you ask will be well informed.

Interviewers are rightly fond of springing questions like 'What did you think of our page five feature?' You can't be expected to have read the paper or magazine all your life but you can be expected to have a sound knowledge of the last few issues. Be prepared to say what you like about it.

Interviewers also like asking you what you would change. Be careful. Of course they want someone who has thought about things, and has an opinion, but if you say the thinkpiece on page seven is rubbish, you will find you are talking to the author. So practise tactful but informed answers like this: 'The think piece on page seven certainly was an unusual take on the subject. . .'

Another favourite question is to ask what you would include in the paper or magazine that is not at present there. Think carefully about this beforehand, look at rival papers and be ready with something. But keep it polite. Not 'Your coverage of rock music is rubbish' but, 'Personally I would like to see another page or two about. . .'

yourself

Think about what you are going to say about yourself. A favourite question is 'Where do you see yourself in three/five/ten years' time?' An answer along the lines of 'Anywhere but here in rural Cumbria' will not go down well. Of course senior people on local papers and small magazines realise that their best young trainees may move on. But remember that you are talking to someone who has made a career in rural Cumbria and is happy with it. You need to word very carefully any suggestion that you don't think they have made the right career choice.

At least one former student, I am convinced, would have got a job on the *Liverpool Post*, if he had not said at the interview that he planned to stay for two years maximum. The news editor of the paper, quite rightly, reckoned he had got a pretty good job, and did not take kindly to being told by a 22-year-old that it wouldn't be worth staying in Liverpool to work one's way up there.

Spend plenty of time beforehand working out what you might be asked to talk about, and what you might be asked to do. It is very important to make sure you are bubbling with ideas and enthusiasm. Don't make your only question the one about pay. You should be able to think up some questions which show that you have done some research: 'How much of an overlap is there between this paper and the rival in the nearby city?' 'I read about the new Japanese electronics factory in the town. That will presumably help with employment prospects?' and so on.

The interview invitation should tell you whom you will be meeting and whether there will be a written test, and so on. If it is not clear, you are entitled to ring up beforehand and ask. There is no point in being put off your stride if, when you were expecting one person, there is a big panel interviewing you.

I once found, left open on a computer, a document showing one former student's research preparing for an interview the next day. She had listed questions the interviewers might ask and what she would reply, questions she might ask, what they might reply, and what next question she would follow up with. It had clearly taken several hours to compile, and ran to several pages of carefully researched material. She went to the interview, and was phoned on her mobile and offered a staff job within ten minutes of leaving the building.

The interview itself

Get there early. If you are the kind of person who is often late, get there even earlier. Dress appropriately: generally, for any mainstream lifestyle or B2B magazine or newspaper, you should be in a suit or the equivalent. For rock magazines or lads' mags dress in the style of the magazine. But it is safer to dress up than down.

Take your portfolio of cuttings/references, etc. But make sure you don't leave it with them, either deliberately or by mistake. Take a few extra photocopies of the best cuttings, in case they have lost the ones you sent with your CV and letter.

Be enthusiastic and charming. It is impossible to overemphasise this. People have often got very good jobs largely because of charm. Body language is important. If you sprawl back in the chair you will look bored even if you aren't. Sit forward, look alert and look the interviewer in the eye. If you find all these things difficult, practise on your friends and family. Don't behave like a politician: listen carefully to the questions, and make sure you actually answer them.

If you feel the interview is going badly, and that they are hinting that you are not quite what they are looking for, ask to do shifts. Explain that you really want the chance to show what you can do.

On the whole be positive about everything you have done so far. If they ask about the work experience that you did last year, don't say it was rubbish even if it was. Find something positive about it and talk about that. If you think the course you have just paid several thousand pounds for was not worth it, keep that to yourself as well. If this is an interview for a second job, again, when asked why you want the new job, don't make the first reason 'because I'm not happy where I am'. For one thing, that is pretty obvious, but it makes you sound so negative. Points like 'I have learned a great deal, but feel I am ready for a bigger challenge' makes you sound a much better prospect. No one wants people who moan: Eeyore is very funny in the Winnie the Pooh books, but would be a real pain to share an office with. This is particularly important in small offices.

after the interview

It is rare for people to come out of an interview thinking that they have given it their very best shot. If you feel you have, fine. But if you feel you have given a poor impression in one area, think about following it up. If you felt perhaps that you had been a bit blasé about the area or the job, when actually you would kill to work there, write a letter and make sure it gets there the next morning (hand deliver if necessary). Thank them for seeing you, and then try to explain concisely what you wish you had said. I have known of cases where people had been rejected for a job, and an enthusiastic letter the following morning changed the managing editor's mind.

If you don't get the job, try to treat the whole thing as a learning experience. Ring up and ask politely if they will explain where you went wrong. Check through your notes. And get the *Press Gazette* and *The Guardian* again next week.

Moving on

Once you are in a job decide to make the most of it. The great thing about journalism is that so many of the skills are instantly transferable. If you can interview a couple about their golden wedding and get a good human story, which gives an idea of what they are like and makes us feel we have met them, then you can interview the prime minister and do the same.

If you can accurately sub and cut to length a story about a new type of plastic packaging for a B2B magazine, you can sub anything. Nowhere is this seen more often than in B2B magazines, where reporters and subs move regularly from one area to a totally different one. You can be working on *Rail News* one minute and *Nursing Times* the next. And from either of these you could move to a big regional or national paper, as a transport or health correspondent.

If you are taken on as a trainee you will probably sign a contract for a fixed period; during this time you can expect the company to spend a bit of money on training you, while in exchange they can expect you to work hard, make a contribution to the publication, and pass any exams you sit. It is not a good idea to break a training contract if a better job comes along, and there have been cases of serious ructions when a trainee has decided to do this. He or she may well find the paper asking to be paid back whatever has been spent on training.

If you have some other kind of contract, say for six months or a year, again, it would be a mistake to try to break it. It is probably sensible to expect to stay in a first job for at least a year, even if there is no training contract, and it would certainly be worth staying longer if there seems to be more to learn.

Some weekly papers almost seem to expect their trainees to move on once they have completed their training contract. Certainly the salaries some of them pay makes this extremely likely. But it isn't a good idea to keep saying you intend to move on. It is far better to become one of those people who wants to do a good job and enjoy it, and wants to learn as much as possible wherever they are. If you are generally interested in people, then any small local story should present a worthwhile challenge. A tribute piece to a former head teacher whom you had never heard of ought to be an interesting exercise in trying to sum her up, give the readers a flavour of what she was like, and also make those who knew her exclaim, 'Yes, she really was like that.'

However, when you do decide to move on, you will probably need to put as much effort into getting the second job as you did getting the first. You may also need to think about your skills. Read the job ads, such as they are, and try to work out whether you are missing some skill that would help you get an interview. Try to talk to people doing jobs you would like, and find out what you need to get one. There are various short courses around which might plug gaps in your skills, particularly in desktop publishing. Some of these short courses are extremely expensive, because often companies pay to send their staff on them. So have a good look around to work out the best value. The National Union of Journalists has started running short courses that have built up a good reputation, and are cheaper than those run by commercial firms.

Some jobs are advertised, so keep a watch on *The Guardian*, the *Press Gazette* and job websites. But there are far more jobs out there than are advertised, and the grander the paper or magazine, the less likely they are to advertise. So it is back to the same plan – brush up the CV, organise four or five good cuttings (**not** originals) and make a list of target publications. Telephone and find the exact name and job title of the person you need to write to. Or of course, if you have some other contact, use that. Remind the news editor about the work experience you did there (if it went well!). If you work for a weekly, and want to move to the evening paper in the area, get to know the reporters, whom you will meet while covering stories, and ask one of them for help or a recommendation. A former student recently got a very good job partly as a result of a very tenuous link I had with a newly appointed editor.

Write your cover letter carefully. It must be eye-catching, it must show what you have got to offer, in terms of knowledge of the geographical area, or knowledge of a particular speciality, or solid desktop publishing skills. If you have got some pages you have designed which are good, send copies of those. Of course you will almost certainly not want to tell your present employer you are applying for other jobs, but if there is someone else, perhaps a former tutor, who might give you a testimonial to put in with your letter, that will be worth including.

Your target publication will almost certainly expect you to do some trial shifts before giving you a job. The bigger the paper, the less likely you are to land a staff job or a long-term contract without working quite a few shifts. So you will need to think about using up some holiday for this. It is not uncommon for young reporters seeking to move to London from the provinces to use up their entire holiday allocation for a year doing shifts at various papers before getting a contract. And if you still can't nail down the job, and are determined to move to London, then it is a case of giving up the job in the provinces, moving to London anyway, and trying to set up enough shifts to keep you going until you land the staff job.

An even bigger leap in the dark, which does come off sometimes, is to simply head off abroad. Several former students have done this. In each case they spent several years working in Britain to get a good solid grounding before setting off. It might be possible to fix up at least contacts or possibly a contract to string for a particular paper. One student worked for two or three years on a financial journal here, to get enough experience to enable him to cover business affairs in Africa, then he bought a laptop and a one-way ticket to Nairobi, and set off. It was hard at first, especially as some publications are so slow and casual about paying freelances. But in the end he was offered contracts with two major news agencies on the same day. He is still there, and happy.

12

Contacts

- *General advice, details of courses and training*
- *Training providers*
- *Prizes*

General advice, details of courses and training

National Council for the Training of Journalists

NCTJ Training Ltd
Latton Bush Centre
Southern Way
Harlow
Essex
CM18 7BL
Tel: 01279 430009
www.nctj.com
Email: Info@NCTJ.com

The NCTJ's site has information about courses which it accredits at all levels, and about its programme of study which leads to the National Certificate Examination.

National Union of Journalists

308 Gray's Inn Road
London
WC1X 8DP
020 7278 7916
www.nuj.org.uk

Many pages of useful information for would-be journalists, including impartial advice about selecting courses, and suggestions for how to judge the many courses available. It also has details of its own training courses, which are mostly aimed at working journalists wishing to expand their skills.

The Periodical Publishers Association (PPA)
Queens House
28 Kingsway
London WC2B 6JR
020 7404 4166
email: info1@ppa.co.uk
www.ppa.co.uk
Very useful advice and information about getting into magazine journalism.

Periodicals Training Council
Same address as above.
02074044168

The Picture Research Association represents picture researchers on all types of publication. Their website, www.picture-research.org.uk has a great deal of useful information about the job and how to get into it.

The Newspaper Society, which represents the regional press, has advice about training on its website, newspapersoc.co.uk

The best-known industry magazine, the **Press Gazette**, publishes an annual supplement in the spring on journalism training, with many useful addresses. www.pressgazette.co.uk

mediaguardian.co.uk has extensive information about the industry, training and jobs.

www.holdthefrontpage.co.uk is a useful site with stories about the press, job adverts and advice about training.

www.journalism.co.uk offers information about journalism and training, and carries job ads.

www.prospects.ac.uk has details about many graduate jobs, although very few or none are in journalism because of the random nature of the journalistic job market. However, there is useful general information, including advice about funding for postgraduate courses.

www.lifelonglearning.co.uk/cdl has details of career development loans.

Association of British Science Writers
Wellcome Wolfson Building
165 Queen's Gate
London
SW7 5HE
Tel: 020 7 439 1205
absw@absw.org.uk
Information about courses for those who wish to write about science.

Training providers

Universities and Higher Education Colleges
The first place to look is the UCAS website:
Universities and Colleges Admissions Service (UCAS)
Rose Hill
New Barn Lane
Cheltenham GL52 3LZ
www.ucas.co.uk

You will apply through here if you are planning to do a first degree. UCAS gives details of the many hundreds of journalism and media studies degrees all over the country. But beware, it is quite hard sometimes to find all the courses available (though there are around 600 courses with the word journalism in the title). Some courses are listed as, for example, multimedia. Some, because they are joint degrees, are not always all that easy to find. It would be best to make a short list of possible universities and colleges, and then research each one thoroughly.

If you find a degree which interests you, try cross-checking with other sites to see if you can work out how well this degree is regarded. Many of these universities also offer postgraduate diplomas and MAs.

The list that follows is not exhaustive, but it includes the best-known higher education establishments.

Bournemouth University offers, among other courses, a multi-media journalism course covering print, broadcasting and online, and was the first in the country to gain accreditation from the NCTJ, the PTC, and the BJTC (Broadcast Journalism Training Council). www.bournemouth.ac.uk

Cardiff School of Journalism, Media and Cultural Studies offers several courses. www.cf.ac.uk./jomec. Cardiff and City (see below) are 'the Oxbridge of journalism schools' according to the *Guardian Media Directory*.

City University, based in Clerkenwell in London, offers two joint undergraduate degrees and several postgraduate diplomas and MAs. All the City courses are very practical, with the declared aim of preparing students for the workplace. www.city.ac.uk/journalism

Goldsmiths College. This college, part of London University, is based in Camberwell in south London. Its several undergraduate degrees seem fairly theoretical, and a postgraduate MA mixes theoretical and practical work.

University of Central Lancashire, based in Preston, offers a wide variety of post- and undergraduate degrees. www.uclan.ac.uk

London College of Printing, which is about to change its name to the London College of Communications, offers courses at several levels, both in various types of journalism and in photography. www.lcp.linst.ac.uk

Liverpool John Moores University offers an undergraduate degree and a postgraduate MA. At the time of writing there was very little information on the website, but presumably more information is available by post. The courses seem fairly practical. www.livjm.ac.uk

Napier University, based in Edinburgh, offers postgraduate and undergraduate courses. www.napier.ac.uk

The Scottish Centre for Journalism Studies, a joint venture between the University of Strathclyde and Glasgow Caledonian University, offers postgraduate degrees, and the two universities independently offer various undergraduate degrees in journalism or related subjects. www.strath.ac.uk/Departments/scjs

University of Sheffield offers postgraduate and undergraduate courses. www.sheffield.ac.uk/journalism

University of Westminster offers post and undergraduate courses, including a degree in medical journalism. www.wmin.ac.uk/mad

There are many colleges of further education offering a variety of courses, from foundation degrees, to postgraduate diplomas, Btech and HNDs. Many of these are listed on the NCTJ website.

Again, this list is not exhaustive, but these are some of the best-known ones:

Cornwall College www.cornwall.ac.uk
Darlington College of Technology www.darlington.ac.uk
Harlow College www.harlow-college.ac.uk
Harrow College www.harrow.ac.uk
Highbury College, Portsmouth www.highbury.ac.uk
Lambeth College, South London www.lambeth-college.ac.uk
Sheffield College, Norton Centre www.sheffcol.ac.uk

There are a number of commercial training organisations where you can expect the fees to be higher than at FE colleges. The quality of teaching and the job outcomes may or may not be better. It is essential to do thorough research before embarking on any course. These centres generally offer pre-entry courses, as well as short introductory or refresher courses for journalists who need extra skills.

The Editorial Training Centre, based at St Leonards-on-Sea, near Hastings. www.editorial-centre.co.uk
Journalism Training Centre, based in Mitcham in Surrey. www.journalism-training-centre.co.uk
London School of Journalism www.home-study.com

NoSWeat Journalism Training, based in Clerkenwell, London
www.nosweat.co.uk
PMA Training, near King's Cross in London www.pma-group.co.uk

Bursaries and awards

What follows is a list of the major awards available for the study of
journalism. However, things may change at any time, so it is worth
asking around and doing plenty of research, in case new awards
spring up.

The **Arts and Humanities Research Board** (AHRB) administers
awards for postgraduate study. For UK residents, the award covers
tuition fees and a maintenance grant. For EU residents, the award
covers tuition fees only. www.ahrb.ac.uk

The **Scott Trust**, owner of *The Guardian* and *Observer*, runs a
bursary scheme – the Scott Trust bursaries – that provides for six
students to take postgraduate newspaper journalism courses at
City University or the University of Central Lancashire. The aim is
provide an opportunity for those who would struggle financially to
study for a career in journalism. The Trust has said, 'We hope that
these awards will encourage graduates from diverse social and
ethnic backgrounds to apply.' For more details look on the
Guardian Unlimited website or contact the universities.
Applications usually close in February.

The **Wellcome Trust-ABSW Bursary** provides eight bursaries,
each worth £10,000, funded by a grant from the Wellcome Trust
and administered by the Association of British Science Writers.
They are intended to help science graduates to undertake
postgraduate training in journalism or science communication.
www.absw.org.uk/bursaries or contact The Administrator, ABSW,
23 Savile Row, London W1X 2NB; 020 7439 1205; email:
absw@absw.demon.co.uk

The **Leach Trust** has established a bursary scheme that will enable
three disabled graduates to study for a one-year postgraduate
course in broadcast production or broadcast/print journalism.
The award will be made to students who have already won a place

on a one-year accredited postgraduate course and who have a disability as defined by the Disability Discrimination Act of 1995. Application form from Mark Weston, Light Leap, 38 Stonehill Road, East Sheen, London SW14 8RW.

The **George Viner Memorial Trust** aims to help ethnic minority students who are on industry-recognised training schemes. Details from the NUJ, which also has details of the Felix Dearden Prize, for an ethnic minority student's piece of journalism 'which contributes towards and gives a fair balanced picture of anti-racism and multi-culturalism in Britain and Ireland'. Details of both awards at www.georgeviner.org.uk.

The **Fred Sillence Bursary** – available to students embarking on a journalism course at Harlow College, Essex is made in memory of former Royston Crow editor Fred Sillence, who died in August 1999. It is worth £500. Details from the Royston Crow www.royston-crow.co.uk

The **John Buchanan Bursary** – available to students on an NCTJ course at the following colleges: Brighton, Crawley, East Surrey, Highbury (Portsmouth) – is a single grant of £100 towards NCTJ training expenses. Details from The Trustees, John Buchanan Bursary, 10 Cricketfield Road, Horsham, West Sussex, RH12 1TE.

In-house training schemes

A number of newspapers, newspaper groups, agencies and other organisations run training schemes, but this list may not be exhaustive, as new ones are offered and others sometimes do not run because of financial constraints.

The *Financial Times*, the *Daily Mirror*, the *News of the World*, *The Sun* and *The Times* have all run training schemes in the recent past. The BBC runs a news trainee scheme (tel:020 7765 0005), as does the Press Association (tel:020 7963 7000), and Reuters, www.reuters.com.

Most of these schemes recruit in the late winter or early spring. It is important to make lists of entry dates and application deadlines. Many also expect applicants to do a fair amount of work, for example studying the publication and writing comments, or preparing feature pitches. So it may well be that you will need to start work on the application long before the final closing date.

Many big regional groups run schemes, among them the Trinity Mirror, (Trinity Editorial Training Centre – 0191 201 6043 tony.johnston@ncjmedia.co.uk), Johnston Press (Johnston Training Centre – 01604 231528), the Midland News Association (www.mnainsite.co.uk 01902 742126) and Archant (www.archant.co.uk).

Training on the many papers owned by Northcliffe Newspapers and Newsquest is generally done regionally. To find out about training opportunities, you should contact the paper on which you want to work. Northcliffe, in association with the *Daily Mail* and the Press Association recently ran a very successful training course for sub-editors, which may be repeated.

Useful guides

Benns Media UK and Willings Press Guide list publications throughout the UK. Both are too expensive to buy, but can be found in libraries.

The *Media Directory*, published by *The Guardian* with regularly updated editions, gives masses of detail and contacts for many publications, as well as up to date information about training opportunities.

Prizes

A good way to get noticed would be to enter for some of the many journalism awards. There are specific ones aimed at students or those not yet employed in the industry. New prizes appear from time to time, and existing ones disappear, so this list is not exhaustive.

Telegraph Young Sports Writer, www.sport.telegraph.co.uk.
The Observer Hodge Photographic Award www.art-directory.net
Guardian Student Media Awards mediaguardian.co.uk various categories
The Sir William Lyons Award for motoring journalism www.guildofmotoringwriters.co.uk

Young Travel Writer of the Year www.travelsouthusa.com or *Travel Trade Gazette*

Press Gazette Student Journalism Awards www.pressgazette.co.uk various categories

The Catherine Pakenham Award: for young women journalists, contact Emma Gilbert-Harris, 020 7538 6257 emma-gilbert-harris@telegraph.co.uk.

The Felix Dearden prize – see under bursaries

Vogue Talent Contest for 'creativity, wit and style'. 0207 499 9080.

NUS Student Journalism Awards run by the NUS (National Union of Students) and the Daily Mirror. nusonline.co.uk

Further reading

As discussed in Chapter 10, for those who want to get into print journalism the most important thing to read is print journalism, as much and as often as possible.

There are a great many 'how to' books around. It is probably best to see which ones course tutors recommend if you are planning to study, and/or to look in libraries at some of the books available, before spending too much money. Journalism is a very subjective craft, and a story that one person thinks is brilliant, will make another cringe. So it follows that one tutor will love a particular book, and another will not like it at all.

Routledge's series of short guides, *English for Journalists*, *Writing For Journalists*, *Interviewing for Journalists* and so on is a good basic introduction. The most essential of these is *English for Journalists*, by Wynford Hicks, (1998) which gives very clear guidance on the most common grammatical pitfalls, and also covers points such as jargon and word economy.

Similar areas are covered in more depth in Harold Evans's *Essential English*, published by Pimlico (2000).

The Routledge 'Handbook' series covers areas of journalism and how to work in them in greater depth. They include *The Newspapers Handbook*, by Richard Keeble, (2001) and *The Magazines Handbook* by Jenny McKay (2000).

Troublesome Words, (Penguin, 2002) by best-selling travel writer Bill Bryson, was first published about 20 years ago, when he was a sub-editor on *The Times*. He's come a long way, and so has the book, which has been revised and updated, and will soon be published again as *Bryson's Troublesome Words*, a recognition by the publisher that the book will sell on his name alone. The book is invaluable for anyone who wants to be sure they have got the correct word for something. He says, tongue-in-cheek of course, that it could be subtitled 'Even More Things in English Usage That the Author Wasn't Entirely Clear about Until Quite Recently'.

Eats, Shoots and Leaves, the Zero Tolerance Approach to Punctuation, published by Profile became a runaway success at Christmas 2003 for its author Lynne Truss, although occasionally her own use of grammar is a bit suspect, and plenty of readers have found her style slightly irritating.

Oxford University Press publishes a series of books called 'One Step Ahead', which cover punctuation, words, editing and so on, and are good accessible little guides.

The Penguin grammar books are also well worth considering, there is a guide to plain English, a guide to punctuation, and a dictionary of grammar.

The Plain English Campaign is an independent organisation that campaigns for clarity in documents from public bodies and firms. Their idea is that these documents should be 'something that the intended audience can read, understand and act upon the first time they read it'. Much of what they advise is exactly applicable to would-be journalists. Their website, www.plainenglish.co.uk has some free material, including an A–Z of ways of making things more concise. Their quotes from the winners of their 'Golden Bull' awards, for English that was anything but plain, make very amusing reading.

Background reading

This list includes some of the most popular books by journalists, and in some cases about journalism. Some are out of print, but can be traced fairly easily through internet book searches. A lot of them should be in college or other libraries.

Investigations

Bower, Tom, *Broken Dreams: Vanity, Greed and the Souring of British Football*, Simon and Schuster, 2003. The renowned investigative journalist and author writes about corruption in top-flight football. Also recommended is his 1996 book, published by HarperCollins, *Maxwell: The Final Verdict*.

Cathcart, Brian, *The Case of Stephen Lawrence*, Penguin, 2000. *New Statesman* and *Independent* journalist investigates the black student's murder.

Coggan, Philip, *Easy Money*, Profile Books, 2002. The markets editor of the *Financial Times* on how easy it is to be parted from your money and how get rich quick scams have changed Britain.

Hale, Don et al, *Town Without Pity*, Century, 2002. The account, by the former editor of the *Matlock Mercury*, of his almost single-handed successful campaign for the release of Stephen Downing, who served 27 years in jail for a murder he did not commit.

Harding, Luke; Leigh, David; Pallister, David, *The Liar: The Fall of Jonathan Aitken*, Fourth Estate, 1999. The story of *The Guardian*'s investigation into the Jonathan Aitken corruption scandal and the ensuing libel case.

Harvey, Graham, *The Killing of the Countryside*, Vintage, 1998.The effects of intensive farming and EC subsidies on the British landscape and rural life. Graham Harvey is agricultural story editor of *The Archers* and for some time wrote as Old Muckspreader in *Private Eye*.

Hitchens, Christopher, *The Missionary Position: Mother Teresa in Theory and Practice*, Verso Books, 1995. The left-wing journalist's attack on Mother Teresa is a fascinating polemic.

Klein, Naomi, *No Logo*, Flamingo, 2001. The bestselling attack on the brand-name culture.

Moore, Michael, *Stupid White Men...and other Sorry Excuses for the State of the Nation!* HarperCollins, 2002. Journalist/satirist's analysis of the US government. Also by him, *Dude Where's My Country?* Allen Lane, 2003. More scathing analysis of the US authorities, including discussion of the reasons behind the decision to go to war on Iraq, and of the Enron scandal.

Monbiot, George, *Captive State: The Corporate Takeover of Britain*, Pan, 2001. *The Guardian* columnist's very readable account of privatisation.

Page, Bruce, *The Murdoch Archipelago*, Simon and Schuster, 2003. An analysis of the media man and his worldwide empire.

Palast, Greg, *The Best Democracy Money Can Buy*, Constable and Robinson, 2003. BBC and *Observer* investigative journalist uncovers political corruption and corporate fraud on both sides of the Atlantic.

Snoddy, Raymond and Ashworth, *Jon, It could be You: The untold story of the UK National Lottery*, Faber, 2000. Behind the scenes politics, rivalries and tensions in the winning of the licence and the running of the lottery, unearthed by *Times* journalists.

Watergate: many books, including:

Bernstein, Carl and Woodward, Bob, *All the President's Men*, first published in the 1970s, with a 20th anniversary edition published in 1994. A classic account of the world's greatest piece of investigative reporting by the reporters themselves. Also, by the same team, *Final Days*, Simon and Schuster, latest edition 1994. The events of Richard Nixon's last weeks in the White House.

Kutler Stanley I., *Wars of Watergate: The Last Crisis of Richard Nixon*, Random House, 1992. Watergate and its legacy for the American people.

Reeves, Richard, *President Nixon: Alone in the White House*, Simon and Schuster 2002.

Garment, Leonard, *In Search of Deep Throat: the Greatest Political Mystery of Our Time*, Basic Books, 2001. Thorough and successful search for the main source of the original Watergate information.

Reportage

Abrams, Fran, *Below the Bread Line*, Profile Books, 2002. Fran Abrams went undercover for *The Guardian* working as a night cleaner at the Savoy. Then she did a month in a Yorkshire pickle factory and a month as a care assistant in Scotland to research this book on poverty and exploitation.

Collin, Matthew, *This is Serbia Calling: Rock'n'roll radio and Belgrade's Underground Resistance*, Serpent's Tail, 2001. The former *I-D* and *Big Issue* editor writes about B92, the anti-Milosevic radio station run by Serbia's 'lost generation' of young people.

Di Giovanni, Janine, *Madness Visible*, Bloomsbury, 2004. Highly acclaimed reportage about the Balkans from the front line war correspondent.

Judah, Tim, *Kosovo: War and Revenge*, Yale University Press, 2002. The former *Times* and *The Economist* correspondent gives a heart-rending eyewitness account of the war in Kosovo.

Kapuscinski, Ryszard, *The Soccer War*, Granta, 1998. Kapuscinski is a Polish journalist who started out working for the Polish Press Agency, which could afford only one reporter in each continent. This meant he travelled to any and every country where there was a coup or revolution. This is an eyewitness account of 20 of them, from Algeria to Namibia, as well as an account of the soccer war between El Salvador and Honduras.

Keane, Fergal, *A Stranger's Eye: A Foreign Correspondent's View of Britain*, Penguin, 2001. The celebrated foreign correspondent turns his attention to Britain for a BBC series, and describes the poverty and exclusion he discovered in Britain at the end of the 20th century.

Garcia Marquez, Gabriel, *News of a Kidnapping*, Penguin, 1998. A journalistic account of the kidnapping of several Colombian notables by drugs barons, by the renowned novelist.

Orwell, George. Any of the journalism, e.g. *The Road to Wigan Pier* or *Down and Out in Paris and London*.

Pattullo, Polly, *Fire from the Mountain The tragedy of Montserrat and the betrayal of its people*, Constable and Robinson, 2000. The science, the politics and the effect of the volcano that destroyed the Caribbean island.

Politkovskaya, Anna, *A Small Corner of Hell: Dispatches from Chechnya*, University of Chicago Press, 2003. Moscow journalist's harrowing book.

Vitaliev, Vitali, *Borders up! Eastern Europe through the Bottom of a Glass*, Pocket Books, 1999. A look at how people in Russia and Eastern Europe have adapted (or not) to capitalism.

Younge, Gary, *No Place Like Home A Black Briton's Journey Through the American South*, Picador, 2000. The *Guardian* journalist explores interracial politics in the southern states of the US.

Collections of journalism

Amis, Martin, *The Moronic Inferno and other visits to America*, Penguin, 1991. Journalism from the acerbic British novelist. Also *Visiting Mrs Nabokov and other excursions*, Penguin, 1994.

Barber, Lynn, *Demon Barber*. Penguin, 1999. Caustic, probing and sometimes confrontational interviews from a mistress of the art of profile writing.

Bernard, Jeffrey, *Reach for the Ground: the Downhill Struggle of Jeffrey Bernard*, Duckworth, 2002. A collection of the best of his *Spectator* Low Life columns. There are also other collections available from this master of the columnist's art.

Burchill, Julie, *The Guardian Columns 1998–2000*, Onion mass market, 2001. Collection of writings by one of the most popular columnists around.

Buford, Bill (editor), *Press: The Best of Granta Reportage*. Penguin/ Granta 1994. Includes John Le Carre, Martha Gellhorn, John Simpson, James Fenton, Ian Jack, Germaine Greer.

Foot, Paul, *Articles of Resistance*, Bookmark, 2000. Collection of pieces from award-winning investigative journalist.

Gellhorn, Martha, *The View from the Ground*, Granta, 1998. Peacetime dispatches – wonderful eyewitness reports, 1936-87.

Greer, Germaine, *The Madwoman's Underclothes, Essays & Occasional Writings 1968–85*, Picador, 1987. Journalism and other writing from the doyenne of women's writing.

Johnson, Phil, *Straight outa Bristol: Massive Attack, Portishead, Tricky and the Roots of trip-hop*, Coronet, 1997. Johnson has been a music critic for *The Independent* and *The Independent on Sunday*. This is his account of the roots of the Bristol sound from the 1980 St Paul's riot onwards.

Jones, Dylan ed., *Sex, power and travel, Ten Years of Arena*, Virgin, 1996. Collection of writing by many well-known journalists from the magazine.

Levin, Bernard. There are several collections of his columns from *The Times*. They are mostly published by Jonathan Cape, and include *Enough Said*, 1998; *I Should Say So*, 1995 and *If you Want my Opinion*, 1992. Levin became one of those rare columnists who was often cited as a main reason for buying the paper. But as his style became increasing idiosyncratic, there were those who found him unreadable.

Lispector, Clarice, *Discovering the World*, Carcanet, 1992. Extremely imaginative personal journalism by a Brazilian writer/novelist.

Morris, Jan, *A Writer's World, Travels 1950–2000*. Faber, 2003. Not travel writing, although the journalism is from all over the world. Much of it describes historic moments. Jan Morris, then *Times* reporter James Morris, broke the story of the ascent of Everest in 1953. *Conundrum*, the story of her sex change, is also worth reading.

Pilger, John, *Heroes*, Vintage, 2001. Or other books by the investigative reporter.

Williams, Richard, *Long Distance Call (Writings on Music)* Aurum, 2000. A collection of pieces on music by this award-winning journalist. Also by him, *The Death of Ayrton Senna*, (Bloomsbury 1999), a biography of the racing driver.

Savage, Jon, *Time Travel: From the Sex Pistols to Nirvana. Pop, Media and Sexuality 1977–96,* Vintage 1997. Collection of essays and music reviews.

Sawyer, Miranda, *Park and Ride (Adventures in Suburbia)*, Abacus 2001. One of those love it or hate it books, an exposure of the absurdities of suburbia.

Smith, Joan, *Different for Girls: How Culture Creates Women*, Vintage 1998. Essays on a diverse range of women from the Princess of Wales and Naomi Campbell to Rosemary West.

Self, Will, *Junk Mail*, Penguin, 1996. Collected journalism on drugs and other subjects.

Wolfe, Tom, *The Purple Decades*, Picador, 1993. A compilation from the work of the journalist described as 'the man who reached parts of the typewriter that other reporters never rumbled'.

Wolfe, Tom and Johnson, E.W., *The New Journalism*, Picador, 1975. A collection of journalism from the USA, 1960s onwards, which eschews the conventional 'Who What Why Where When' and goes for every other offbeat style.

Wurtzel, Elizabeth, *Bitch*, Quartet, 1999. Essays on women behaving badly from former music journalist and author of *Prozac Nation*.

autobiography

Cockburn, Claud, *I, Claud*. Out of print but available secondhand. Extremely funny autobiography by radical journalist who worked for *The Times*, and later wrote for *Private Eye*. He died in 1981. The book doesn't, to be honest, tell us much about what it is like on a national newspaper today, but it gives a witty portrait of a more spacious relaxed newspaper era.

Diamond, John C., *Because Cowards Get Cancer Too....* Vermilion 1999. John Diamond was the best-known of several journalists who wrote about their own fatal illness.

Evans, Harold, *Good Times, Bad Times*, Weidenfeld and Nicholson, 1994. Autobiography by former *Sunday Times* and *Times* editor about his distinguished career at *The Sunday Times* and short-lived and turbulent editorship of *The Times*.

Parris, Matthew, *Chance Witness: An Outsider's Life in Politics*, Penguin, 2003. The autobiography of the gay former conservative MP, columnist and broadcaster, who outed Peter Mandelson on TV.

Simpson, John. Several volumes of memoirs, including *News From No Man's Land: Reporting the World*, Pan 2003.

Journalists on Journalism

Chippindale, Peter and Horrie, Chris, *Stick it up your Punter!: the Uncut Story of the Sun Newspaper*, Pocket Books updated 1998. Analysis of the rise of the *Sun*, home of arguably the best and worst of British journalism, and how the paper rewrote the rules of tabloid journalism.

Greenslade, Roy, *Press Gang*, Macmillan, 2003. Lively study of the British press.

Knightley, Philip, *The First Casualty: The War Correspondent as Hero and Myth-Maker from the Crimea to Gulf War II*. Andre Deutsch 2003. Updated analysis of war reporting by award-winning investigative journalist.

Stott, Richard, *Dogs and Lamposts*, Metro Publishing 2002. Stirring times on *The Mirror* by its former editor.

Travel

Bryson, Bill, *Notes from a Small Island*, Perennial, 2001. Satirical look at Britain through American eyes. Or other books by him, e.g. *The Lost Continent*, which was his first big bestseller.

Buford, Bill, editor, *The Best of Granta Travel*, Penguin/Granta 1991. Travel writing by some of the great names in journalism.

Vitaliev, Vitali, *Little is the Light: Nostalgic Travels in the Mini States of Europe*, Pocket books, 1995. Post-Soviet reports from the witty Russian journalist.

Analysis/Politics

Granta 53 News, Granta Books 1996. This edition of the literary magazine takes news as its subject.

Alibhai-Brown, Yasmin, *Who do we think we are? Imagining the New Britain*, Penguin, 2001. Investigation into the public and private spheres of multi-racial Britain.

Hitchens, Peter, *The Abolition of Britain*. Quartet, 2000. An indictment of Blair's Britain from a rightwing perspective by *Express* columnist.

Hitchens, Christopher, *No one Left to Lie to: the Triangulations of William Jefferson Clinton*, Verso, 2000. A critical look at Bill Clinton's presidency and Hillary Clinton's senate campaign.

Marr, Andrew, *The Day Britain Died*, Profile, 2000. A look at the future of the nation by former *Independent* editor.

Paxman, Jeremy, *The English: A Portrait of a People*, Penguin, 1999. By the *Newsnight* presenter. Also by him, *The Political Animal*, Penguin, 2003.

Fiction

Far and away the best novel about journalism is Evelyn Waugh's *Scoop* (1938), which has never been matched. Anyone aspiring to be a journalist should read this hilarious book, not least because some of the characters, particularly Lord Copper, a thinly-disguised satire on Beaverbrook, and the hapless reporter William Boot, have entered the collective sub-conscious.

Michael Frayn's *Towards the End of the Morning* (1967) is also extremely funny, and a terrific portrait of Fleet Street in the 1960s, now disappeared forever under the gleaming new merchant banks and law offices.

The Shipping News, (1993) by E Annie Proulx, is one of those books which people seem to either love or find a bit irritating. Its description of small-town journalism, though the people are sometimes caricatures, rings true.

Heartburn, by Nora Ephron was first published in the US in 1983. It is a very funny, wry account of the break-up of a marriage between two journalists. Ephron wrote, among other things, the screenplay of *When Harry Met Sally. Heartburn* was not published in the UK originally, but in 1998 became available here, published by Pocket books. Don't be put off by the awful and extremely unfunny film version.

Films

For an evening in front of the video or DVD player there are several films about journalism.

By far the best is *All the President's Men*, 1976, director Alan J Pakula, starring Robert Redford and Dustin Hoffman. Well-made and exciting thriller about Watergate, based on the book by the two investigative reporters (see above).

The Year of Living Dangerously, 1983 director: Peter Weir, starring Mel Gibson, Sigourney Weaver. Indonesia in 1965, the time of the massacre of up to 500,000 people. Bit too much of a feel of Hollywood about this, and the journalist characters are fairly obvious, but it gives some idea of what it might be like to be a foreign correspondent.

Under Fire, 1983, director: Roger Spottiswoode, starring Nick Nolte, Gene Hackman. The Nicaraguan revolution seen through the eyes of journalist Russell Price.

The Insider, 1999, director Peter Mann. Al Pacino, Russell Crowe. True story of journalist and whistleblower taking on tobacco industry, but pretty short on characterisation.

The Front Page. There are several film versions of this 1928 play by Charles MacArthur and Ben Hecht about an unscrupulous newspaper boss's attempts to prevent his ace reporter from leaving. The 1931 version by Adolphe Menjou is reckoned by film buffs to be better than the 1974 Billy Wilder version, which starred Walter Matthau and Jack Lemmon. Then there is the Howard Hawks version of 1940, *His Girl Friday*, which stars Cary Grant and Rosalind Russell as a female version of Hildy, the ace reporter.

There are also various plays: in particular *Pravda* by Howard Brenton and David Hare, which has a great portrait of a press baron who merges two papers which sound very like *The Sun* and *The Times*. Soon after the play was staged at the National Theatre, the papers and their respective Sunday versions moved en masse to the same plant at Wapping, so it almost came true.

Michael Frayn's *Alphabetical Order* is quite funny. Tom Stoppard's *Night and Day* is not one of his best, and the journalists are very much stock characters.

Glossary

ABC: Audit Bureau of Circulation, which provides independent official figures for sales of publications.

Ad: advertisement.

Add extra material, perhaps provided by a different reporter, which will be added to a story.

Ad-ed ratio: the relationship between the amount of advertising and editorial in a publication.

Advance: copy of a statement or speech issued to the press before it is made.

Advertisement feature: editorial material that has been written as part of a package to go with some advertising, sometimes known as **advertorial**.

Agony aunt: columnist, usually a woman, who collates and writes replies to readers' worries about personal issues. There are a few agony uncles around.

Angle: the way a story is written to give a certain slant to it. Papers with conflicting political stances will often adopt totally different angles on the same story.

Art editor: senior person, usually on a magazine, who is responsible for the design.

Artwork: pictures, graphics or other material ready for the printer.

Assignment: a job on which a reporter or photographer is sent.

Attachment: 'the journalism of attachment' is a late 20th century expression, referring to the theory that when reporting conflicts journalists have a greater responsibility not to make matters worse than had perhaps been acknowledged before. A related expression that is probably gaining more currency is **peace journalism**. This phrase was first used in the 1970s, but the theory is becoming much more widely discussed now. It suggests that reporters need to think and write more about conflict resolution than just conflict.

Attic: the material across the top of a page. On the front page of a newspaper it can refer to the 'puffs' or 'sells' across the top above the masthead, which highlight various stories to be found inside.

Backbench: group of senior journalists with final responsibility for what gets into a paper, its design, and for getting it to press on time.

Background: essential material which needs to be in a story (usually fairly low down) explaining how the event came about, or the issue arose. Thus a backgrounder is an extra story containing this material.

Bagging: the practice of enclosing a magazine (or sections of a weekend paper) in a plastic wrap. It might hold sections together, or keep a cover mount attached to the publication.

Banner: a headline which runs right across a page.

Basement: a story which runs across the bottom of a page, often lighthearted. It is important for the overall design of the page.

Beat: two meanings: one news provider might beat another in getting a story; in the US it also means the subject area covered by a reporter (science/health/environment, etc). In Britain these reporters are generally referred to as specialists.

Bleed: running material, usually a picture or design feature, to the edge of the page.

Blob: black dot, square or maybe star at the beginning of a paragraph. Sometimes used with a short related story placed at the bottom of a longer one. Following computer jargon, it is sometimes known as a bullet point.

Body: the main part of a story, excluding the headline.

Book: slightly old-fashioned term referring to a publication. Thus, material appears near the front or the back of the book and a 'tight book' is one with a lot of ads and therefore little space for editorial.

Box: extra material related to a main story and placed in a box (i.e. with a frame around it, perhaps also with a tinted background). It might be a chronology, 'ten things you didn't know about X', or some extra facts about an event or issue.

Break: a story breaks when it first becomes known to the press.

Breaking story: one which happens while a publication is about to go to press.

Break-out: extra material, such as facts, chronology, advice, perhaps included in a **break-out box** or **fact box**.

Brief: details given to reporters, feature writers or photographers to enable them to start work on a story.

Broadsheet: large format newspapers such as *The Financial Times*.

Bullet see **blob**.

Bureau: name for the office of a news agency.

Bury: to leave some important point too far down a story. This expression took on new meaning with the infamous email about burying bad news on 9/11.

Business to business or B2B: magazines about a particular industry, for the people who work in it.

Byline: the name of the writer of a story, usually included at the top.

Calls: routine visits or phone calls to various news sources that reporters make regularly, e.g. to the police and fire service.

Campaigning journalism: name given to journalism that in its exposure of injustice or wrongdoing, seeks to right a wrong.

Caption: line of information under a picture, usually a photo, explaining its significance. A caption story refers to a slightly longer piece combining a short story with the caption.

Casual: journalist working on a day rate, usually for a newspaper. This person is doing casual shifts, or is said to be shifting.

Cast-off: calculating exactly how long a story will be when laid out on the page.

Catchline: single word that identifies a story to enable it to be traced in the system.

Centre spread: material placed across the centre two pages of a newspaper or magazine.

Chequebook journalism: the practice of paying people in the news to get exclusive interviews with them.

Chief sub: the leader of the team of sub-editors.

Circulation: the number of copies of a publication that are sold.

City desk: the desk that covers financial and business affairs. This comes from the British expression 'City' meaning the financial centre of London. In the US the city desk would be the one covering the affairs of the city in which the paper is based.

Classified ads: small advertisements, often for property, jobs and cars.

Colour piece, colour writing: editorial material that gives a picture or flavour of a place or event.

Column: first person opinion or anecdotal piece.

Commission: a features or news desk will commission a freelance to write something. On magazines this is often the main role of the **commissioning editor**.

Compact: the name the shrunken broadsheet papers are giving themselves, to avoid being called tabloids.

Conference: meeting that takes place once or twice a day on a paper, or less often on a weekly or monthly magazine, to discuss which stories and pictures will be used, to monitor progress and possibly also review the previous issue.

Consumer magazine: a publication carrying material about leisure interests and purchases.

Contacts: people a reporter contacts to find out material. A good reporter will keep in contact with large numbers of people who may be able to help with information.

Contacts book: the book, or personal organiser, or both, in which a journalist stores the phone numbers of every contact.

Contract publisher: a firm producing magazines on behalf of other organisations, such as charities, pressure groups or businesses.

Controlled circulation: refers to magazines, usually B2B ones, that are distributed to a particular group of people working in a specific sphere.

Copy: journalists' term for the words they write.

Copy approval: arrangement when a publication agrees to allow an interviewee, or the subject of a piece, to see the material before publication. Some celebrities insist on this.

Copy-taster: senior sub-editor or backbench person who looks at all incoming copy from staff reporters, agencies and freelances and decides what will go into the publication or onto the wire at an agency.

Cover lines: attention-grabbing headlines on the cover of a magazine which advertise what features are inside.

Cover mount: item such as a CD, or sachet of shampoo attached to the front of a magazine.

Cover price: the price at which a publication sells to the public.

Credit: photographer's or artist's name appearing with their material.

Crop: cutting a picture down to exclude unwanted background.

Crosshead: short phrase, or even a single word, appearing within the body of text to break it up for design purposes.

Cross-reference: important line at the bottom of a story drawing the reader's attention to a related story, column or leader elsewhere in the publication.

CTN: confectioners, tobacconists, newsagents, traditionally shops where magazines and papers are sold.

Curtain raiser: forward-throwing story written before an event takes place.

Customer magazine: publication, possibly free, supplied by large businesses or other groups to their customers or subscribers.

Cuttings: two meanings: the previous stories about an issue, now held electronically, but which used to be cuttings from the publication stored in a cuttings library. Also known as **cuts**. Also refers to the stories which a journalist has had published and has kept copies of in a portfolio.

Cuttings job: critical term for a report or feature based entirely on stories that have appeared previously.

Dateline: place from which a story was written, usually abroad. If an agency issues a story with a certain dateline, it indicates that it has a reporter there.

Deadline: the last moment by which a story or page must be ready.

Deathknock: an assignment when a reporter is sent to try to talk to the family or friends of someone who has died.

Deck: a headline, usually used when there might be two headlines to a story, in different types. This would then be a two-deck headline.

Delayed drop: the practice, often on a featureish or humorous story, of leaving the main point of the story until further down the story. Also known as a **drop intro**, or, by older hacks, a **slow burner**.

Diary: two meanings: on a newspaper the list of events, sometimes kept in a desk diary, or possibly now electronically, which the news editor hopes to get covered. It also means nowadays various different types of light-hearted gossip columns.

Diary item: a piece for inclusion in a diary column.

Doorstepping: the practice of a reporter arriving unannounced outside someone's house or place of work in the hope of getting an interview. Reporters sometimes spend days outside a newsworthy person's home.

Downtable subs: the rank and file sub-editors who edit copy at the request of the senior team.

Drop cap: a larger sized capital letter at the beginning of a paragraph.

Dummy: two meanings: it can mean a mock-up booklet of a publication, which shows where the main advertisements are. It also means one or more issues of a new or potential publication which are practice runs and can be shown to investors, advertisers, focus groups and the like.

Editorial: two meanings: all the written material in a publication and also the **leader**, the column expressing the considered view of the editor.

Embargo: a note on a speech or statement that explains that it is not to be used until a certain time.

EPD: electronic picture desk.

Exclusive: a story that no other publication has got, a **scoop**.

Exes: expenses.

Eyewitness: a piece by a reporter at the scene of an event.

e-zine: magazine issued only on the internet.

Factbox: material, usually in a frame, which gives some extra information which would be too indigestible in the main story.

Fanzines: magazines, usually about sport or music, written by enthusiasts who are not expecting to make any money out of the venture.

Feature: this term now covers the vast amount of material that is not about news. Features might be anything from background pieces, interviews, information about products to buy, recipes etc.

File: the action of sending a story in for publication, often used in agencies.

Filing editor, filer: a senior agency journalist responsible for sending the copy to the subscribers, or putting it on the wire. Filers will decide which subscribers should be sent a story, and whether it rates a snap or a flash.

Filler: short story used, especially on small regional and local papers, to fill up a gap in the page.

Fireman: reporter (male or female) on an agency or newspaper who is sent immediately to cover a newsworthy event.

Flam up: to hype up or oversell a story, which then perhaps turns out not to be so good.

Flannel panel: the column in a magazine giving the names and perhaps contacts of the staff.

Flash: the fastest, briefest dispatch from an agency used only for a very important story. It will be followed almost immediately by a fuller version. See also **snap**.

Flatplan: a large sheet with boxes for each page which the senior editorial team will use to decide where to place various stories.

Fleet Street: term still used for Britain's national press, although they have all left the area.

Fluffy: describes a light-hearted, perhaps humorous feature.

Focus group: people brought together to discuss a new or existing magazine or product.

Font: a particular style of type.

Follow-up: a new story, with new material, written about something that was covered in a previous edition or rival publication.

Fourth Estate: the press. This expression, which has been attributed to the 19th century historian Thomas Carlyle, seems to have been used first by Edmund Burke in the 18th century. It refers to the fact that the clergy, lords and commons make three estates, but the press is also a power in the land.

Freebie: a free outing, lunch, holiday, or product given to a journalist, in the hope of positive publicity.

Freelance: journalist who does not have a staff job, but who writes, probably for several publications, and gets paid for the material used.

Freesheet: or simply **free**, newspapers which are distributed free.

Galley proof: a paper showing the words of a story, before they have been arranged in a page layout. It dates back to the metal tray, or galley, in which the lines of lead type were held.

Gatefold: a page that opens out from a magazine, usually carrying an advertisement.

Ghost writer: a journalist who does most of the writing of a book or a comment piece. The journalist 'ghosts' a sportsperson's 'autobiography' or writes a piece for a politician who is invited to contribute to publication.

Go to bed: go to press, when the publication is sent to the printers and nothing further can be changed. **Offstone** means the same thing, and refers to the heavy metal benches on which the pages, made up of lead type, used to be put together. Both 'go to bed' and 'offstone' are now rather old-fashioned.

Graphics: illustrations including charts, maps, diagrams almost always now computer-generated.

Grey market: advertising term for older people.

Grid: newspapers and magazines used to be designed on a fairly specific grid giving a set number of columns to a page. This is less necessary now with the arrival of new software.

Gutter: the central margins between two pages.

Hack: journalist, possibly a derogatory expression, but in fact journalists themselves seem happy with it.

Hamper: a story displayed horizontally, often across the top of the page. See **basement**.

Handout: press release or other item from which a story might be written.

Hard copy: a print out or paper version of a story.

Hard news: items about politics or other significant events.

Heavies: term referring to the broadsheet papers. It is not used so much now, as they get lighter.

Hold over/out: used when copy does not get into a publication for one of many reasons, but is not **spiked**, so it might be used in the future.

Hole: journalist's term for a vital piece of information missing from a story.

House ad: an advertisement placed by the publisher in one of its own publications. House ads are sometimes used when at the last minute a story is seen to be unsound.

House journal: a publication produced by a firm for its own workforce.

House style: certain ways of using punctuation, modes of address, etc, which a paper or magazine has fixed on. New recruits should obtain the house stylebook and make a point of referring to it when in doubt.

Human interest: a rather vague expression denoting a story about the interesting doings of a person or group of people, but which may have no long-term significance.

Infotainment: new word coined to describe the many stories in newspapers, especially at the weekend, which appear to be newsworthy, but are in essence simply entertainment and have no lasting significance.

Insert: some copy that is put into a story later, perhaps for clarification.

Intro: the first paragraph of a story.

Inverted pyramid: used to describe the traditional way of writing a news story, with the important information at the top, and then the rest of the material arranged in descending order of importance.

Investigative reporting: although all journalism involves finding things out, this term is generally taken to mean the practice of looking very closely at an issue or event, and trying to piece together exactly what happened, or is happening, and why. Investigative reporters will sometimes, perhaps not often enough, uncover frauds or injustices.

Kill: when a story is not used in the publication it is killed. Agencies use this expression on an urgent message when they realise that a story which has been issued is incorrect. Magazines and newspapers pay a kill fee to a freelance if a piece has been commissioned and then not used.

Knock down: when one publication runs a story disproving something in a rival.

Landscape: a picture or graphic in which the horizontal measurement is longer than the vertical one, as opposed to an upright.

Layout: the design of a page or pages.

Lead: two meanings: lead pronounced as in 'take charge of' is the main story in a paper or magazine, or the main story on a page (page lead); lead as in the metal refers to the practice of putting extra space between lines of type – the space used to be provided by inserting strips of lead in the metal type trays.

Lead-all: see **round-up**.

Leader: see **editorial**.

Legal: (verb) to arrange for a lawyer to check a story for potential libel or contempt.

Lift: taking a story, possibly from a rival publication, and using it, perhaps with minimal changes.

Lineage: the rate paid to a freelance, when it is based on the length of a story.

Literal: this expression used to refer in the past to errors during the printing process. They are also known as typos (typographical error). Since journalists are now responsible for their own material as it appears in the paper, these errors are perhaps more realistically regarded as spelling errors.

Lobby: group of political journalists who are allowed into the members' lobby (and bar) of the House of Commons and therefore have privileged access to MPs. They are also invited to various briefings with politicians.

Logo: the title of a magazine as it appears on the front, and possibly in other promotional material.

Masthead: strictly this is the device appearing above a paper's leader column, and **titlepiece** refers to the name on page one. However the two words are often used interchangeably.

Me-column: a column about the writer's own doings, from going to the supermarket or getting the washing machine repaired, to putting the baby to bed.

Middle-market: generally taken to refer to the *Daily Mail* and the *Daily Express* and their associated Sunday papers.

Mug shot: head and shoulders front facing photograph.

New journalism: literary, perhaps rather mannered, form of writing which has become popular in the United States.

Newsdesk: the group of journalists responsible for organising news coverage.

Newsletter: highly specialised B2B publication aimed at one area, generally a financial one. They are almost always entirely financed by the subscription fee, and have no advertising. They are now usually distributed eletronically.

NIB: News In Brief, generally a selection of short stories run down one column.

Night editor: senior production journalist on a morning paper who takes control when the editor goes home and is responsible for getting the paper out on time.

Night lawyer: a lawyer who works in a newspaper office, or is available on the phone, to check stories for legal pitfalls.

Nose: (old-fashioned) term for the intro to a story. To **re-nose** a story would involve writing a different intro.

Obit: obituary, an account of someone's life published soon after his or her death.

Off diary: stories which reporters discovered for themselves through observation, or possibly contacts, which have not come through the obvious news sources such as the police or a council.

Offstone: see **gone to bed**.

Off-the-record: when a source reveals some information on condition that it is not attributed to them.

On spec: sending a freelance piece to a publication although it wasn't commissioned. Generally rather a waste of time.

Op-ed: the page Opposite the Editorial page, where usually a newspaper carries political columns and other commentaries.

Opinion piece: article expressing the writer's own opinion. This would generally refer to a one-off piece. If a publication carries a regular article by the same person, it becomes a column.

Orphan: see **widow**.

Overline: headline, generally in smaller type, appearing above the main deck of a headline.

PA: the Press Association, Britain's main national news agency.

Package: a group of related stories and pictures that will be arranged together in a publication.

Par: paragraph.

Paparazzi: photographers who make their living out of getting unauthorised pictures of celebrities.

Pay-off: the final line, perhaps jokey, in a feature or light-hearted piece. Known to some older hacks as the **kicker**.

Peace journalism: see **attachment**.

Peg: sometimes also called the nut of a feature. It is the point when the writer explains the answer to the question 'Why am I telling you this (now)?'

Photomontage: illustration, often jokey, which uses superimposed photos and possibly other material.

Picture byline: a small photo or drawing accompanying a writer's byline.

Picture desk: the group of people who assign the photographers, commission freelances and research picture sources.

Pocket cartoon: small, single-column cartoon, often on the front of a newspaper.

Pool: arrangement whereby a few journalists are allowed to cover an event, perhaps a royal tour, and they then share their material with others.

PR: public relations, the team within a firm or other organisation who work to make sure that press coverage of the organisation is favourable.

Press release: an announcement to the press, probably now released electronically.

Production editor: the person who coordinates the work of getting a publication to the printer. He or she will work with a **production schedule**.

Profile: a reflective piece, usually about a person in the news, but it might sometimes be about an organisation, generally giving life story, background, etc.

Proof: a paper version of a page or pages produced in time for it to be checked through. Hence also the verb to proof.

Publisher: in magazines, the senior person responsible for the overall financial management of the publication.

Puff: two meanings; it can refer critically to a piece which presents something in a very favourable light, and therefore might be biased. It also refers to the promotional pictures and headlines, generally on the front of a newspaper, which advertise stories inside.

Pull-quote: a quote, drawn from a story, and printed in larger type, perhaps in a box. It is used partly to catch the reader's eye but also sometimes to break up a large area of type.

Ragged right: (or more unusually, **ragged left**) unjustified type.

Readership: the number of people who read a publication, which is usually a much larger figure than the circulation.

Red top: tabloids such as *The Sun* that have red mastheads.

Re-jig: rewrite a story.

Reportage: descriptive writing or photography that seeks to give atmosphere and a picture of an event or situation.

Retainer: sum paid to a freelance to ensure that she will provide copy.

Retouch: to alter a photograph, now done electronically.

Returns: unsold copies of a publication returned to the publisher.

Revise sub: senior backbench person who has a final look at copy before the page is finally passed.

Ring-round: when a team of reporters conducts a telephone poll of a particular group, say MPs or doctors, asking their opinion about a current issue.

Rip-out: major remake of a page between editions.

Round-up: a story which incorporates material from several different reporters or agencies, also called a wrap or, on an agency, a **lead-all**.

Running story: a news story in which a series of events unfolds, or facts become known, so that the reporter, especially if working for an agency, has to rewrite and update the story several times.

Scoop: see **exclusive**.

Screamer: very old-fashioned term for an exclamation mark in a headline.

Serif: small strokes at the ends of letters, in type such as Times New Roman. **Sans serif** type, such as Arial or Verdana, lacks them.

Sell: a sentence or two in larger type at the top of a feature, intended to lead the reader into it. Generally magazines use the word sell, and newspapers use the word **standfirst**.

Set left (or right): a headline set to the left hand margin of a column.

Sidebar: an extra story relating to the main one, often placed in a **box** on the same page.

Silly season: towards the end of July and during August, when there are generally fewer newsworthy events, newspapers are reduced to carrying increasingly inconsequential stories.

Sister paper: used to refer to two papers, owned by the same firm, which were similar. Now of course, the *News of the World* is the sister paper to *The Sunday Times*.

Sketch: a light, often humorous piece of writing describing an event, especially the sittings of House of Commons.

Slotman/slotperson: the person in an agency bureau who is responsible for giving a final check to stories before they are filed to head office. The slotperson equates to a news editor on a publication.

Snap: agency term for a very brief item alerting subscribers to an event. It will be followed by a more detailed story. For the most dramatic event the agency will issue a **flash**.

Snapper: jokey term for photographer.

Soft news: light stories that do not have any great significance.

Spike: unused material in newspapers and agencies used to be placed on a metal spike, so it could be retrieved if necessary. The term is still in use in some computer systems. From that the verb **to spike**.

Spin-doctor: press officer or other communications person whose job it is to make sure favourable material appears in the media.

Splash: the main front-page story in a newspaper.

Spoiler: when one newspaper has paid someone in the news for the exclusive rights to their story, a rival paper, usually a tabloid, might run a spoiler attacking that person, and seeking to discredit their testimony.

Spread: a story running across two facing pages.

Standfirst: see **sell**.

Staffbox: see **flannel panel**.

Strapline: see **overline**.

Stringer: a freelance who has contracted to provide coverage for a publication. Often the stringer will be paid only for what the publication uses. A **super stringer** will usually have a slightly more favourable arrangement, perhaps being paid a retainer.

Stylebook: – see **house style**.

Sub-editor or sub: one of the team checking stories for content, accuracy, legal pitfalls and style, cutting them to length, and writing headlines. Some will design pages.

Tabloid: small format newspapers such as *The Sun*. See **compact**.

Teaser text: a phrase used sometimes in magazines, but particularly used now for internet journalism, referring to the phrase on the home or other page that persuades the surfer to click on it to get the whole story.

Think-piece: personal opinion or analytical piece.

Tip-off: when someone, perhaps a member of the public, or a freelance, gives some information that will be useful to a journalist. Publications will sometimes pay a tip-off fee, even if they want to follow up the story themselves.

Top: a story appearing at the top of a page.

Upright: see **landscape**.

Vox pop (*vox populi*): the practice of interviewing random people, probably in the street, about an issue.

Whistleblower: a person within a company who leaks information to the media to the discredit of the company.

Widow: a short line at the end of a paragraph which, when the story is put into the page, appears at the top of a column. It looks ugly and subs are asked to avoid these. An **orphan** is a similar short line at the bottom of a column.

Wire: agency term for its service. To wire means to send in material, usually pictures.

WOB: White On Black: material, usually a headline, that is in white characters on a black background. Hence also BOT: black on tint.

Wrap: see round-up.

Epilogue

'The life of journalists is often a dog's life. When others sleep, they work. Where others have definite hours and well-defined duties, there is no limit to the calls that a newspaper may make upon those who slave in its service. Journalism is not a comfortable profession. It is full of dangers, drawbacks and disappointments – but it gives some of the highest satisfactions for which a human being can hope.'

Henry Wickham Steed (then editor of *The Times*)
to students of journalism, University of London, 1921

Index